The COLORS of FREEDOM

Immigrant Stories

By Janet Bode

Franklin Watts
New York London Hong Kong Sydney
Danbury, Connecticut

This book is dedicated to these remarkable teachers:

Erminia Claudio, William A. Morris Middle School, Staten Island, New York
Patricia Power, Teacher Academy, Edinburg, Texas

Visit Franklin Watts on the Internet:
http://publishing.grolier.com

Library of Congress Cataloging-in-Publication Data
Bode, Janet.
    The colors of freedom : immigrant stories / by Janet Bode.
        p. cm.
    Includes bibliographical references and index.
    Summary : Newly arrived teenaged immigrants describe their experiences in America, recount traditions of their native countries, and present short stories, poems, recipes, and artwork. Also provides interviews with native born American teenagers who share their family histories.
    ISBN 0-531-11530-5 (hardcover)
    ISBN 0-531-15961-2 (soft cover)
    1. Minorities—United States—Miscellanea—Juvenile literature. 2. Immigrants—United States—Miscellanea—Juvenile literature. 3. Minority teenagers—United States—Miscellanea—Juvenile literature. 4. Teenage immigrants—United States—Miscellanea—Juvenile literature. 5. United States—Emigration and immigration—Miscellanea—Juvenile literature. [1. Minorities—Miscellanea. 2. Immigrant—Miscellanea.] I. Title.
E184.A1B587 1999
305.8'00973—dc21   98-29608
                                                                    CIP
                                                                    AC

GROLIER
PUBLISHING

What's Inside

The Journey

1

Writing a book is like going on an adventure. What discoveries you'll make and how they fit together don't become clear until you reach the journey's destination.

I invite you to come along.

New York City.
March fourth, a year ago.

I'm on a ferry crossing the New York Harbor on my way to meet a seventh-grade journalism class at Morris Middle School on Staten Island. The thirty-two students and their teacher, Erminia Claudio, are ready to discuss how best to help me with the research for the book I'm writing.

They know the topic, our nation's shared immigrant experience. When we get together later that day, I'll explain more about my main goal: to collect the stories of our newest residents, people from different countries who now call the United States home. I also want to learn how those born in this country answer some basic questions: Who am I? What part of the world did my ancestors come from? And how do I feel about the recent arrivals?

I look off in the distance to see both the Statue of Liberty and Ellis Island. Since 1886 Lady Liberty has been holding her famous torch, offering the welcoming words "Give me your tired, your poor. . . . I lift my lamp beside the golden door!" To this day immigrants from around the planet accept her invitation.

Ellis Island has long filled an equally important role. From 1892 to 1954 it served as the gateway to the United States for immigrants, primarily those from Western Europe. Today forty percent of Americans have at least one relative who first stepped ashore there.

Early in the twentieth century on peak days as many as 5,000 hopeful immigrants were poked and questioned by teams of officials deciding their fate. Within view of their American Dream, some were denied entry and forced to return to their homelands. Even now if you visit this site, you can almost hear their cries of pain.

In 1990 the main buildings opened again, this time as a museum. Walk inside and suddenly you time-travel to generations ago. There are old photos and weathered clothes, passenger tickets and an enormous pile of steamer trunks, remnants of yesteryear's relatives, donated by today's family members. I wonder, what kind of a nation would we be now if those people hadn't been willing to set sail for America? And what is it today's immigrants bring to the mix?

Suddenly the ferry docks and I'm off on step one of my journey, Morris Middle School, Staten Island, New York. But more about that later.

STEP TWO, STEP THREE

Back home at my computer, I send e-mail to Patricia Power and her ninth-grade students at Teacher Academy. They come from such adjoining towns as Edinburg, Pharr and San Juan, all quick rides from the U.S. side of the Texas–Mexico border. The immigrant issue is something they live with daily.

I've asked them, too, if they'd be interested in contributing to this book. In previous e-mail, I agreed with their teacher's suggestion that they intellectually fly with the idea of immigration and

roots and see where it takes them. In a heartbeat, Power e-mails me back.

Date: Wed, Mar 5, 6:27 PM EST
From: PPower
Subj: Approval for Project (Teacher Academy) Granted
To: Janbode
Hi, Janet.
The principal has approved the cultural awareness project. The students' participation will be on a volunteer basis with parental approval. It's full steam ahead.

Next I contact Halbe Dougherty-Wood, a junior at Vashon Island High School, located off the coast of Seattle, Washington. Although there are school districts in the United States where more than a hundred languages are spoken, in her school the situation is the reverse—English only. Nearly all the students' families are a couple of generations removed from European roots.

Halbe tells me about a survey done by the school paper staff about the student body's lack of racial diversity. The article reads, "Overall students fear that the isolation will leave them with a feeling of ignorance toward people from other cultures with whom they will interact in the future."

She also mentions an American Studies assignment to write a paper on "What It Means to Be an American." I'd like to see those essays I tell her.

E Pluribus Unum, One out of Many

As the months pass, I travel to schools around the country. "Please write about your roots," I tell the students. And they do. One day I feel I'm island-hopping as teenagers from Haiti, Puerto Rico and Trinidad let me enter their lives. Other days it's as if I'm exclusively in the former Soviet Union or Asia, South America or Africa. Then I'm on to small-town America with hardly a recent immigrant in sight. In time I have collected nearly 1,000 mini-autobiographies, intimate slices of real life.

Along with those short accounts, I begin to conduct one-on-one interviews. The first is with a girl from the South American nation of Guyana. Up front I let these individual students know that to protect their privacy, I'll change their names and certain telling details.

For me and for you the reader, I want to find out how we are different, how we are the same and what we can learn from one another. With this girl we start with a description of daily life in her motherland and end with her hopes for the future. Just before she leaves the room, she suggests I call her Shazeena, the name of her best Guyanese friend. I like that.

Then I ask, as I always do, "Is it okay to phone you with any further questions?"

"No problem," she says, disappearing into the packed hallway of a school with 4,000 students. She was raised in a village with a population of 400.

Suddenly, though, she stops, turns around and comes back. "I am just one girl," she says, "one set of eyes looking at my country. Each person from Guyana is different. Let the readers know that, please."

I know she's right.

How can I capture and portray a whole culture through a lone individual? Life in a remote farming community, for example, is going to be different from life in a dense urban sprawl. Add to that the fact that the role of a male and a female in the same culture can be worlds apart.

American Mosaic

Those who share their stories serve as a starting point. From them you get a longer look at one life, combined with a glimpse of the country of their birth and its traditions and rituals. You also begin to understand the realities of the immigrant experience.

To try to discover a bit of the breadth of a culture, Patricia Power's Teacher Academy students in Texas show the way. At the end of May boxes arrive containing more than fifty of their cultural awareness projects. They take my breath away.

Date: May 30, 10:18 PM EDT
From: Janbode
Subj: Breathless
To: PPower

As I went through each project, I kept interrupting my partner, Stan, a cartoonist, saying, "Wow! Listen to this. Look at that." Racism from a teen's eyeview, riveting poetry, spiritual beliefs and superstitions, folk remedies. I felt as if I were gathering pieces with which to create an American mosaic. . . . Janet

CELEBRATION OF CULTURES

Around the same time I return to Staten Island's Morris Middle School to discover how they've decided to approach this topic and to collect what information they've gathered. The teacher, Erminia Claudio, has turned the room into a celebration of cultures.

On long tables are student folders, each containing at a minimum the student's picture, a personal profile and an interview with a recent immigrant. Some of the seventh-graders have done even more, including sweet recipes, mementos from much-loved relatives and elaborate diagrams of family trees stretching back to the 1800s.

Together the class developed an immigration survey and had other stu-dents, parents and neighbors complete it. I make a note to send it to other schools, especially the one on Vashon Island in Washington.

RISK TAKERS AND THE DESPERATE

By late fall I begin to sort out what I'm learning about today's immigrants. Certain patterns appear: The fabric of their family life is often torn apart. A parent comes first. Then as much as a decade later the children follow, and the families try to stitch their lives together again.

The children attend their first day of school, a potentially scary experience under the best circumstances. In their case, they don't have a clue what to think, wear or say. Usually they don't even know the language. When they aren't ignored by U.S.-born students, they are ridiculed. These newest residents are in culture shock, touched by a past they can't forget yet determined to weave it into an American future.

The risk takers and the desperate cross our borders legally and illegally. Some find their American Dream turning into a nightmare—lives overwhelmed by poverty and violence. Others begin to succeed. Whatever the definition of their daily existence, most continue to speak of the value of faith, family and perseverance.

Just like, I imagine, my ancestors did when they first arrived in this country.

13

KNOW-NOTHINGS

Both my parents' families came to America from Germany about one hundred fifty years ago. Their aim? The same as many of today's arrivals—to escape famine and war and to secure a better life in a world they knew only by reputation. All of them settled in Wisconsin around 1848, the same time it officially entered the Union as a state.

I know little of my relatives' early days, but history tells me a political party called the Know-Nothings feared immigrants were taking U.S. citizens' jobs. More restrictive anti-immigrant laws was their answer.

Did my family feel the sting of that negative attitude or were they too busy exploring the countryside around them? I began to wonder. Did they come in contact with the very first residents, members of any local Native American nation? Maybe they would have been more welcoming than descendants of the earlier immigrants.

And how do today's Native Americans feel about the immigrant issue? I decide to ask one last series of

#1 *My great-great-great grandfather, Julius Bode, who arrived in the United States at age four in 1849*

#2 *My great-great-great stepgrandmother, Ida Grassler Bode, born in 1858 in the U.S.*

#3 *Their son, Ernest Bode*

questions. I call John Teller, the former Tribal Chairman of the Menominee, most of whom still live in Wisconsin. He tells me about his culture and says he'll help set up an interview with one of the middle-school students from their reservation school.

WEBSITE

December through March, the hard part. Making the book.

My work space is jammed with piles of real-life short stories, individual interviews, cultural awareness projects, surveys and snapshots of students helping along the way. It's too much to fit into only 150 pages.

I dream of a website.

Scan in everything and invite students nationwide to contribute. I envision a vibrant combination of ethnic music, descriptions of cultural traditions, countless flags waving and then dissolving into the U.S. red, white and blue. The colors of freedom.

Back to reality, I make the choices to create the book you now find between these covers.

ECLECTIC COLLECTION

While you can read this book from start to finish, better yet, think of it as an eclectic collection of journal entries,

memorabilia and a family album. Dip in and out looking for fun, surprises and connections to your own life, family and experiences.

You might turn first, say, to the short descriptions students wrote about their relatives who came here generations ago, as far back as on the *Mayflower*—or on slave ships. Or maybe you're curious about teenagers with roots in the Caribbean island nations. That section could be where you begin your reading. You might want to jump in at the Longer Look sections, oral histories of life in such faraway places as Burundi and Korea. While exploring these stories, remember that the words you read are the words I heard. They may not always be grammatically perfect, but I believe they're always clear.

Still others of you may want to start by matching your opinions of what it means to be an American with those of your peers. And finally, throughout this book you'll find recipes from different parts of the globe. They reflect the joy of one generation sharing with the next the ingredients of a favorite family food. (However, one student confessed that, gee, her grandmother might have left out a secret ingredient—on purpose. Keep that in mind if you try to duplicate any of those treats.)

The final chapter is interactive. Fill out the immigration survey. Take the citizenship quiz and answer the questions that today's immigrants must respond to before being able to swear allegiance to the United States. And then against this broad backdrop, with this clearer perspective of current immigration and the people involved, discuss what you think immigration should be like in the future.

Two Important Notices

1. Most of the students who contributed to this book wish to be anonymous. Therefore, their true identities are hidden behind made-up first names. Sometimes, though, you'll see a complete identification, first and last name. This means that these people agreed to go public and let you know exactly who they are.

2. It's exciting—and on occasion a touch embarrassing—to see your name and thoughts in print, moments frozen in time, now for all to read. Remember, the words reflect the contributors' feelings when they were two years younger. Also, because of space limitations, I often had to shorten their work. For that I'm sorry, but still I know that the power of what they say will touch your soul.

THE COLORS OF FREEDOM

A Family Album
of Those Who Helped

2

SAY CHEESE

In this high-tech world, when I visit
schools, I run a low-tech operation. A dis-
posable camera is one of my tools. While
groups of students write about their past
and their present, I snap away. Here are
some of those pictures, as well as class
photos taken by Erminia Claudio and
Patricia Power and ones contributed by
students themselves—hanging out at
school, on a quinceañera invitation,
from a day at the Texas-Mexico border.

Mr. and Mrs. José Rosbel Martínez
request the honor of your presence
to celebrate the Fifteenth Birthday
of their daughter
Veronica Martínez
on Saturday, April 5, 1997
Triple City Ballroom
San Juan, Texas
Dance: 7:00 p.m.
to 12:00 midnight
Music by
Grupo Xzito

The Rio Grande from the photo-essay A Day at the Border by Annie Ralph, Teacher Academy, Texas.

IN THE BEGINNING

3

Stories from Mayflower Ancestors to the Early 1900s

A NATION OF NATIONS

1565 Spanish soldiers and priests establish the first successful European outpost in what will later become St. Augustine, Florida, in the United States.

1607 English settlers establish the permanent colony of Jamestown, Virginia.

1614 Dutch settlers establish their first major colony near Albany, New York.

1619 African indentured servants first arrive in Jamestown, Virginia.

1620 Pilgrims land the *Mayflower* at Plymouth Colony, Massachusetts.

During the next one hundred fifty years British Catholics; Jewish refugees from Brazil; German, Swiss and Dutch Mennonites; and French Protestant Huguenots come to these shores by choice, along with depressingly large numbers of African slaves forced here to meet the demands of future owners.

Because of restrictive immigration laws, until the mid-twentieth century, most of those who chose to immigrate to the United States were from Western Europe.

Here is a look at the link to the present from these long-ago residents, the first newcomers in a colorful, continuing chain.

Short Stories...

Abigail Carpenter,
Teacher Academy, Texas

While doing research on the genealogy of our family, my great-aunt Mil discovered the last will and testament of William Carpenter, an ancestor who died in 1698. He came to America on the *Mayflower* and settled in Plymouth Colony. He and his family later moved to Rehoboth, Massachusetts, where he died.

Back in those times the distribution of property and possessions was recorded in great detail. Special attention was paid even to minor things such as books, clothing, wool and sugar.

What is willed to loved ones is an important part of any culture. Here are excerpts from the descriptions of worldly goods William Carpenter divided among his wife, six sons and their sons, and his two daughters, one of whom was, like me, named Abigail:

"In the name of God Amen, I William Carpenter, Sr. of Rehoboth, being in perfect memory at present, blessed be God, do make my last will and Testament. . . .

(4) I give to my son William the young grey mare, or two yearling colts, and five pounds in sugar or wampum, and my (passett) coate, and one suit of apparel. . . .

(5) I give unto him my Latin books, my Greek grammer, and Hebrew grammer, and my Greek Lexicon, and I give to him 10 (or 5) pounds of cotton wool; and to his son John, twenty shillings to be paid to him a year after my decease. . . .

(9) I give to my daughter Hannah one yearling heifer, also I give Hannah her Bible, the practice of piety and the volume of prayer, and one ewe at the Island, and twenty pounds of cotton, and six pounds of wool. . . .

(11) I give to my daughter Abigail, one young mare, a three-year-old bay mare, and if the mare should be dead at Spring, she shall have fifteen pounds in her stead, within one year after my decease. . . .

(14) I give to my wife the other half of the land I now live upon, her lifetime, and the use of my household stuff, carts, and plows, if she marry not. . . .

Spelling, capitalization and punctuation are reproduced as found in the original will.

Christopher

During the late 1600s my mother's relatives came to the New World from Holland and Germany. They settled in what was to become North Carolina and Virginia. My father's great-grandfather was that family's first arrival. He jumped off the side of a merchant marine ship in the New York Harbor at the turn of the century. He went on to farm in Upstate New York, log in the northwest United States and marry an immigrant from Palermo, Sicily. That's part of Italy.

Tracy Swinton Bailey,
Language Arts Teacher,
Socastee High School
Myrtle Beach, South Carolina

My Roots
Slaves. Some of them were slaves.
Captured, bought and sold.
Warriors. Still others were warriors
Battling with pride for a land,
a life, a legacy.
Kings, Queens, herbalists, preachers,
Healers, crusaders, beauticians, singers.
My people have spanned the globe—
Covered the spectrum;
But I have not seen their faces
Nor spoken their names.
The legends buried beneath
The nothingness of forgotten time
Leave a void burrowing deeply into the
Consciousness of soul.

Peggy

My father's father—my grandfather—was from Ireland where the only work he could hope for was on a farm. He came from a large family and had a sixth-grade education. He saw his future in America and came here at twenty. He drove trolley trains his entire life and loved it. My grandmother's relatives came from Germany.

My mother's father—my other grandfather—was from Eastern Europe. I don't know which country. When he was in the military medical service, he met and married my gramma. She was French Canadian and lived in Canada most of her life.

Michelle Faulhaber,
Teacher Academy, Texas

My great-grandparents were born in Austria. When my great-grandmother (1887–1981) was nine years old, she was "farmed out" to a wealthy family for whom she cooked and performed other chores. In 1904 my great-grandfather (1883–1973) boarded a vessel in Glasgow, Scotland, and arrived in the Port of New York 13 days later. He traveled by freight train as far as New Mexico, then turned back east to work in meat packing houses and farm. In 1917 he resumed his trade as a butcher and sausage maker.

Daymeon

I am an African-American male, born and raised in Brooklyn. My mother was born in Harlem. So was my father. My grandmother and grandfather were born down South. My great-grandparents were slaves. They were taken against their will. Both grandmothers were raped and beaten when they were young ladies. It hurts to know that.

I have a sister who is nineteen and in her second year of college. I love my life because my parents are the best and will help me have a future.

Aimee Buckner,
Language Arts Teacher,
Brookword Elementary School,
Snellville, Georgia

My great-grandfather came to America from Poland as a "fugitive." (He was involved in a bar fight and left the country.) He also left behind someone of great importance, his girlfriend. The girl's father was pleased.

Two years passed and the father arranged for his daughter to marry. On the eve of her wedding, my great-grandfather returned from America. They eloped and immigrated here in the early 1900s—or so goes the family story.

Matthew

My grandparents on my mother's side lived the life of the English. They ate English food, drank tea and kept to themselves. My grandparents on my father's side were the first generation born in the United States. They were taught by their Polish-born parents to be "American," even though they never stopped speaking Polish at home.

Daisy

My grandfather was an American success story. He came to this country from France as a nine-year-old with his widowed mother and two other sisters. He had been sick and walked with a limp. At Ellis Island he almost didn't get by the doctors. Once here, though, he went to school, learned English, married, had three children including my father, went into the clothing business and was grateful to be in this wonderful country.

Marielena Gallucci,
Morris Middle School, New York

I'm 100 percent Italian. My grandma shared many memories with me. She remembers the Depression and coming to America in 1935 on a well-known ocean liner, the *Rex*. When she was my age, it was 1939–40. She remembers she played jump rope and helped her mother around the apartment. Also, she had to roll knitting yarn into balls for her mother.

Her favorite songs were "Beautiful Dreamer" and "My Blue Heaven." Her favorite singer was Bing Crosby. Her favorite actor was Clark Gable. There was no TV at the time.

When she was in the ninth grade, her principal held an emergency assembly. He said, "The USA has joined World War II." Most of the boys who were juniors or seniors were drafted or signed up for the army.

My grandma took both business and commercial classes. She also helped fill out forms for students who only spoke Italian. That is how she met the man who became my grandpa. In 1949 my grandma was the only female in her college insurance class. She went on to become one of the few women on Staten Island to open her own business, an insurance agency.

The World in Three Parts

PART ONE

Longitude 180° W to 40° W

Stories of the Americas and the Caribbean Nations

4

COMMON BONDS

In telling who they are and where they come from, many students also choose to write about issues that can touch others' lives—regardless where their roots are planted. The details in these stories may remind you of our common bonds with people everywhere.

Short Stories . . .

Marisol

I am from Chile, a long and beautiful country in South America. I remember my neighborhood and the crowded streets of Santiago, the capital city. I remember refusing to come here because I loved my country so much. My mom helped us to understand that life in the United States was our best choice.

Now I am here two years and I like it very much. In the future I see myself as an extremely busy fashion designer. Of course I want to get married, have a baby boy and give him everything I can. I also want to get a good, handsome husband to share all my love with in my extra time if I have some.

—art by Patricia Mosqueira (Peru)
ESL Student, Locust Valley Jr./Sr. High School
Locust Valley, New York

Fanny

I came from Colombia when I was nine years old. I am now seventeen. Colombia is about machismo. Macho-men demand to control everything. To the naked eye people think I have this great life. In school I'm the best student a teacher can have. In reality my father constantly drinks. He used to beat my brothers and sister bloody—and call us all the names in the book. They're married now and I'm the only one left.

Now he comes home and beats my mother. Every weekend it is the same thing. I lie in my bed, hugging myself, afraid to do anything about it. He wants us to be dependent upon him. I tried to get a job, but he doesn't want me to.

Anthony

My mother and father come from the West Indies, while I was born in the United States. Now my grandparents have moved in with us because their home on the Caribbean island of Montserrat is being threatened by a volcano. My life is being put on hold. I have to cook and clean. I have no personal life at all. When you come into my house, it smells like Vick's Vapo-Rub and feet. What am I going to do?

Rafael

My grandmother—my mother's mother—has raised me since I was three. For that reason, I know more about her family and heritage than my father's. My mother's family came here from Cuba during the 1960s. They were part of one of three large migrations from Cuba, known as the Freedom Fighters. They were against Castro, the leader of that country.

Sara

I was born in Argentina. I always dreamed of coming to the United States, and my dream came true on May 6. Before that I felt miserable because I never had a complete family. My father left my mother and me when I was two years old. He came to America to build our future. After ten years I saw him again.

My happiness is school. When I get home, I feel lonely. My friends are my thoughts. My future is my husband. I dream of graduating from college and making me and my family proud.

—art by Patricia Mosqueira

Karina

The reason we have come to America from El Salvador is due to the political unrest and the poor economic opportu-

31

nities that exist in my homeland. However, there isn't a native Salvadorian or visitor who doesn't realize that El Salvador is one of the most beautiful lands that human eyes have ever seen. The beaches, sunsets, fruit trees and culture of this little country are splendid.

There are rural and urban areas just like here. The natives of El Salvador are Indians, like the Native Americans. Then there were the Spanish conquerors who came and Christianized and colonized the country. They also intermarried with the native Salvadorians. That is why our skin ranges from white like the Spaniards to darker—mulatto.

Delia

My parents came to the United States from the Dominican Republic when they were both teenagers. My sisters, brother and I were born here. I am an individual who doesn't care about what people think or say. I have ideas for a better future.

I am compassionate, understanding and can do whatever I put my mind to. I am a poet and will probably become a writer. I don't like school, but I will go to college.

Jesse Briones,
Teacher Academy, Texas

My hometown, Donna, Texas, in Hidalgo County is located in what was territory originally granted to Lino Cavazos on May 19, 1834, by the Mexican state of Tamaulipas. The Cavazos family inhabited the area for at least twenty years, and their descendants continued to live there into the twentieth century.

The first known Anglo-American settler was John F. Webber, who, accompanied by his wife Sylvia, a former slave, settled in the area in 1839. The Webbers moved here to escape persecution for their interracial marriage.

Several families from northern states settled the area, including Thomas Jefferson Hooks. He arrived in the Lower Rio Grande Valley in 1900, purchased land and gave part of it to his twenty-one-year-old daughter, a divorcée named Donna.

Alexandra Aguilar,
Morris Middle School,
New York

I am 13 years old. My favorite hobbies are drawing and ballet dancing. My religion is Mormon. I don't go to church, but I read all the books.

I was born on Staten Island, but my parents were born in Chile. I am the youngest child of seven. Each of us visited Chile when we were younger. I still remember that trip, the food, their customs and the rocky roads. My parents teach me their traditions and I hope someday to teach them to my children.

How to Make Sopaipilla

Alexandra Aguilar,
Morris Middle School,
New York

Ingredients:
5 pounds of flour
1 tablespoon of baking powder
1½ pumpkins (whole fresh ones cut up in little squares)
1 quarter pound of lard or shortening
dash of salt
corn oil

Directions:
Pour flour onto a table that has a smooth surface. Add the baking powder and lard. Boil the pumpkin in saucepan. Let it cool for a while. Then add the pumpkin to the flour mixture and knead the dough well on the table until it no longer sticks to your hands. Spread the dough flat with rolling pin. Cut out round shapes with a cup. Stick each of the shapes of dough with a fork three times to prevent them from bubbling while you cook them. Pour some corn oil into frying pan and fry the round shapes until they are crispy. Let them cool on paper towels to drain oil and pat them dry. Eat with tea, coffee or hot cocoa.

Essay

What It Means to Be an American

Derek,
Vashon Island High School,
Vashon Island, Washington

It is normal and American to be whatever, whoever or anything you want to be. I'm glad there is no way I know of to describe an American. That means to me there is no true red-white-and-blue way I could just pick one person to put on display to show a foreigner what is an "American."

It seems that now Americans come in all different shapes, backgrounds and especially personalities. I guess that's why people say there is a world—or nation—of difference.

A Longer Look:

Interview with Shazeena, a fifteen-year-old girl from Guyana

•••

Guyana, on the northern coast of South America, is the continent's only English-speaking nation.

Imagine. A life built on coconuts. Most people on my island look for work picking coconuts and making coconut oil. Some make a little money planting rice, too.

My father picked coconuts. He climbed to treetops, took a special knife and cut them down. My mother said he always came home sore.

My brother said my father complained about the government. This caused him problems. He wasn't involved that much, but they didn't like the way he voted either. He was thrown in jail. That scared me. He got out and left for the United States.

I was only a child, a few years old. In my family adults don't tell the children much of the present or the past. Generations ago, I don't know when—maybe even a hundred years—my ancestors lived in East India, in Asia, and then came to Guyana. Many East Indians made this same journey. I saw that just by looking at my village.

ANIMALS FIRST

My parents had seven kids, six boys and me. Sometimes the boys ask my advice.

35

"Shazeena," they'd say, "how do you deal with adults if they tell you something and you can't stand it?"

"Live with it" was my best answer in days gone by.

In Guyana we went to public school, but still we had to wear uniforms. A long blue dress with a white shirt for girls. For boys blue pants with a white shirt tucked in.

Me and my brothers made book bags from canvas material and lined them with an old plastic tablecloth. We put our books and shoes in them for the walk to school. The principal would be standing by the gate, ready to lock it. Sometimes when I was late, I'd tell her I had to care for my animals first.

"So did I," she'd say, "and I'm here on time." I'd go get a rag to dry my feet, put on my shoes and enter the school. It was a large room with blackboards to divide the classes. We sat side by side on wooden benches.

WASHING MACHINE WOMEN

Boys don't have to do anything in the home. They just play around. It bothers me. Girls have double the responsibility.

I had to help with the housework, clean, do the dishes, do the laundry—by hand. That's right. Women are the washing machines. We do the cooking, too. In our village stoves are made from mud. To make them hot, I first had to get wood to make a fire. I know the feel of the heat on my body.

My mom raised me until I was eight, and then she went to help my dad in the United States. After that my aunt raised me. I lived with her, my cousins and my brothers.

I hadn't seen my father forever. We didn't have a phone. Nobody did in our village. We would go to a place where there was a phone. I talked to him maybe once every few months. Afterward, I would look at his picture and cry. I wouldn't tell anyone. When my mom left for America, I would cry to her picture, too.

One day, though, when I was twelve, my aunt told me, "I have a great surprise for you, Shazeena. You and your brothers are going to see your parents in the United States." I was so excited I cried without looking at their pictures. Then I thought to myself, I don't know my dad. And Mom's just a whisper of a memory.

"There are two suitcases for all of you," my aunt said. "You can each bring one favorite thing." It was hard to choose what to bring and what to leave when I had so little. My yellow and white dress, I decided, and carefully packed it.

A LION

I flew from my old life to a new one. I remember thinking, My future is going to change totally. My mom and my dad were at the airport. But I didn't even know that man was my father.

Then he said, "My baby girl's grown up so much."

"Go ahead," Mom said. "Hug your father."

By then everybody was crying and hugging. It was our happiest day.

My parents took us to our new home, an apartment in a building with five floors. The tallest building in our village had two floors, upstairs and downstairs.

When I went in, I stared at everything. They had a TV. I knew it was a TV, but I was surprised they had one. In the village there were no televisions. We didn't have regular electricity. Maybe once a week we got some for a while. They had water from a faucet, too. I couldn't believe you could have those things, things to make regular life easier.

My parents wanted us to start school right away. On a Monday, four days after I came here, I went to school. My mom showed me how to cross a street with a light, then waved good-bye at the school door. I went inside alone. The kids were laughing and pointing at me. In my culture the lion is important. I thought about how strong a lion is and I felt stronger.

As time passed, I was still surprised at the differences between here and my island. Here I had to go to school every day. At home our life is part of nature. I know what it means when birds don't sing, the wind comes up,

there's a full moon. Sometimes there is flooding and a tide covered the dirt roads. We couldn't pass for weeks and so we had no school.

I had a lot to get used to in America.

YESTERDAY'S SHADOW

Two years after I first came here, something—surprise!—special happened. I met an Indian boy, Balraj, from Guyana. He was a friend to my brother. He came to visit our home, and we saw each other.

In my culture and in my family, I am not allowed to date. I would be told not to pay attention to him. My parents don't know, but now I sneak out to see him. He wants to marry me. He wants to talk to my parents, except they would be more than angry. I went behind their back.

I see Balraj three times a week. Usually he is outside after school. That makes me smile. We go eat something. We talk. I say, "Why are Indian parents so strict?"

"That's the way they grew up back home," he says. "They live today in yesterday's shadow."

Then I have to go. I have a four o'clock curfew. My mother calls from work and asks, "Shazeena, where were you? Why are you late?" I make up a story.

My father told me he would pick the guy I marry. I tell him, "That is not your choice."

He says, "If you marry someone else, if you spoil yourself that way, I'll kick you out of the family. Forever. Your first brother's marriage was arranged. Your marriage will be arranged."

In my country, by fourteen or fifteen girls are getting married. I'm fifteen now and I'm ready.

LOSING YOU TO AMERICA

Most nights I don't sleep well. I listen to the sound of car alarms, traffic and sirens. I think about what kind of parent I'm going to be: not too strict or too easy.

In the morning I move as fast as I can. All nine of us want to use the one bathroom. There is no system. I don't eat anything before school. No one notices. When I come in, I talk to the security guards, then go to my locker.

That's where I keep my makeup so my father won't know. There's a mirror inside. I put on lipstick and gloss, eyeliner, sometimes black or lime green nail polish. (I take it all off at the end of the day.)

My life is more complicated than when I was a child. My father and mother are stricter than my friends' parents. I can't get and make phone calls. I can't dress any way I want.

"You don't show us enough respect," they say.

"I just want more freedom," I answer.

"We are losing you to America."

It's hard to live pulled apart by what to believe: to balance two cultures yet stay true to my heart.

THE PERFECT FUTURE

I'm curious what's out there in the rest of America. I have never traveled beyond my neighborhood. I'm so glad I'm here. I get more opportunity. I know there's a job somewhere for me.

Ten years from now, I want to have my own home and Balraj, the guy by my side that I want to marry. I want a job working with a lawyer or something like that. I want my future to be just perfect.

A Longer Look :

An essay about Juana, a forty-year-old woman from El Salvador

•••

El Salvador, on Central America's Pacific coast, is bordered by Guatemala and Honduras.

BY PATTY GUIZAR, TEACHER ACADEMY, TEXAS

People move to the United States for many reasons. A common one is to seek a better life. Many will even risk their lives for a taste of freedom.

Juana, her husband and their two children left El Salvador because of war. There were murders every day. The army raided people's homes, hunting and gunning down men they thought were guerrillas, revolutionaries fighting against the present government.

Many innocent people were killed. Juana even saw her neighbors murdered. In a desperate attempt to save her life as well as the lives of her family, they illegally fled to the United States. For one step of their journey they had to cross the Gulf to Mexico by boat. The boats were small and overcrowded. People who could not fit in them had to hang on the side in the freezing water. That is what Juana and her family did.

None of them knew how to swim. Her two sons, ten and twelve years old, drowned. Once in Mexico, Juana and her husband traveled by truck and by train. They ferried across the Rio Grande.

When they arrived in the United States, they wanted to catch a freight train to Virginia to be with Juana's brother and his family. But the Immigration and Naturalization Service (Border Patrol) arrived too quickly. While trying to flee, Juana and her husband became separated. Her feet were blistered and bloody. She was suffering from anemia and malnutrition. She could not get away.

Taken to a detention center in Bayview, Texas, she received medical attention. Because she came from a country at war, where, if returned, she would be killed or locked up as a political prisoner, she met the requirements to apply for asylum to remain here.

And how is Juana doing now?

She said she never could have imagined what a heartbreaking price her family's bid for freedom would cost them. She grieves for her children, and to this day she has not found her husband.

A Longer Look :

I like to write sad poems and short stories. The other day I was making up a person who could have been an ancestor. I called her Martha.

She was born in Africa and before her death, she left behind a story that went something like this:

SENTENCED TO DIE

One night Martha, waking to a fire, tries to run to safety. Suddenly, though, she finds herself with a rope around her neck tied to other tribal members. They are marched to a ship filled with strangers and are chained inside. The air is thin. It smells of feces. Many die from diseases.

On landing, Martha is sold in an auction to a too-friendly master. There is near rape. Shock. A knife. His death. Martha is caught and sentenced, sentenced to die.

This is the story of bondage.

In real life my great-great grandmother was from Africa. I don't know where. My great-great grandfather was born in England. They built their future on the island of Jamaica.

41

LAND OF OPPORTUNITY

I was born in the city of Kingston seventeen years ago. I haven't seen my father, let's see, since I was five. I don't remember how he looks. I don't even have a picture of him.

I lived with my mother until I was seven. Then she moved to America to find a better life for herself and for me. I was left with my great-uncle and great-aunt, my mother's father's brother.

All my friends on the block were like that. Diane's mother went abroad, so she lived with her older sister, who was out of college and working. There was Charlene. Her father went to America to support her. My best friend was Carrie. Her mother went to England. Like me, Carrie's aunts were to raise her.

We all thought of America as a land of opportunity. A place you could do things. Some people, I thought, took this too far. One girl said, "Even if I fail in America, I'll just have a child and live off welfare."

I was a little kid. I missed my mummy. My aunt was a miserable lady, always complaining about something. Where we lived was small. I only had half a room, part of the dining room and the hallway to the bathroom. In the middle of the night someone was always stumbling around waking me.

Plus, to get to my bed, I had to go through my aunt's room. She would say, "Omar, you walk through too much. Omar, you're bringing dirt into the house."

My aunt and uncle favored their own children. The younger one would tease me and the older would hit me. Sometimes I'd try to retaliate, but then I'd get the blame for starting trouble. When I was eight or nine, I told my mother, "They've pushed me to the edge. Mummy, please take me away."

I knew she wanted to have me with her, but it was still impossible. And no one else could care for me.

HOW TO BUILD A LIFE: SPARKY

I built a life of my own. I remember walking to the bus stop too early one morning. This man saw me. He held me up with a knife and took my lunch money. Another time, coming home, these four older kids took my watch. I told myself, "Going through things like that alone makes me a stronger person."

I didn't have any heroes, so I tried to be one for myself. Each time I attempted something, I pushed to do better.

Like with my fish. In my spare time I decided to raise them. I made a file for each one. If a fish got sick, I wrote that down and what I did for treatment.

One breeding season, I had over a thousand. I took many of the new ones to the pet store and exchanged them for pumps and fish food. An angel fish, a male with a big fluffy tail, was my favorite. I named him Sparky. Where he went, the others followed.

RICHARD AND ASTRAN

At home and on the street I spoke Jamaican patois. At school we were supposed to speak English. I'd look for my friends, Richard and Astran. We'd eat breakfast together. I might have hot chocolate and bread with ackee salfish. I think it's called salted codfish here. Some days I'd have porridge or just cold cereal and orange juice.

Richard was the second brightest in our class. He was cool and popular. He was from a different part of the island, not Kingston. He had to get up way early, leave the house at five, get a bus from there to Kingston and transfer to another bus. Astran was the brightest of all. He was unbeatable. I was, maybe, seventh.

We were competitive in academics, but most boys looked more at the sports. We didn't have American football; we had soccer and basketball. I played both of those.

School was split into three courses: the arts, business and science. When you started out in ninth grade, they gave you all the subjects—that's fifteen. Here you usually have the same thing each day. There you have different subjects on different days. The only two that are consistent are math and English.

Mondays we had worship. The whole school went to the hall. It was an Anglican service; that's like Episcopalian. It's a public school, but in Jamaica it's okay to pray in school although you don't have to.

Sometimes I'd pray that I would be living with my mother again. When she called, she'd say, "I miss being there for you the most of anything. As soon as I finish college we'll be together."

A TOTAL SHOCK

I came up to the United States this past summer, expecting to go back. My mother had just gotten her citizenship. One night the end of August, she said, "Omar, you're not going back to Jamaica."

It was a total shock. I went to bed that night and thought, This is a dream.

After ten years apart, I had things planned. I wanted to graduate with my friends and stuff like that. The next day I said to my mother, "Why didn't you tell me?"

"The idea just came to me," she said. "But I understand. You can go back for one week."

With school out I only had a chance to see my closest friends. I went down my street: Diane, Charlene, Carrie. Carrie cried when I told her I was going to America to be with my mummy. "Here, take Sparky," I said to her, hoping maybe that would help her stop crying. I took the rest of the fish to the pet store. I had to leave everything behind.

By the time I got back, my mother had tried to get me in a magnet high school. "They said it was too good a school for a Jamaican boy," she told me. "They put you in the nearest school."

"That's disrespectful," I said, but I went where they put me. And the first day of school was living hell. I didn't know where to go. I didn't know anybody to ask. It was like the other kids spoke a different language.

COVERED WITH LOVE

I missed my friends. I kept calling them until the bill was $200. We talked about everything. There had been a celebration and these people called *johnkanoo*—that's an African word—dressed up and went dancing around the streets scaring little kids. We laughed about how once I ran away from them in terror.

There was an election for prime minister going on. For the first time in history nobody got killed or injured. Usually that's what would happen. My friends said it was peaceful. I felt torn between the two countries.

I tried to weigh which was better. In Jamaica the only attention I got was when I was sick. Even then there were no hugs. Here in America I have a nice family, including my stepfather. I couldn't ask for a better dad. But I don't have friends, I thought to myself.

Still, all those years, I missed my mother. She covers me with love. She's here with her sweet teasing. I'm proud of her and what she's accomplished.

Without her there never would have been me. I am thankful for what I have.

FOOTPRINTS IN THE SAND

I'm trying to get used to life here. I don't understand why if you don't do your homework you get another chance. In Jamaica that's an insult to the teacher. Here, though, I've been exposed to a new world of mathematics. That's what I think I want to do, not be a marine biologist, my earlier dream. I'm doing well in school.

I have a room of my own.

I can close my door.

I have privacy.

I can listen to my music, my rap, alternative, calypso, reggae, soca, rock and roll—without disturbing anyone.

On one wall I have a poster of Julius Irving. On the other are two more. One is an African poster that says KNOWLEDGE IS THE FUTURE. The second is of footprints in the sand. Do you know that story?

A woman had a dream she was walking on the beach with Jesus. She saw her footprints and His in the sand. Then when she was going through a hard time, she saw only a single set of prints. When she asked God why, He said, "That's when Jesus was carrying you through your troubles."

Now once again in my life, there are two sets of footprints in the sand.

A Longer Look :

Interview with Toro and Alen, two fifteen-year-old boys from Dominican Republic

• • •

Dominican Republic, a Caribbean nation, shares the island Hispaniola with Haiti.

Toro:

I'm Dominican. I was born on the island of Hispaniola, what the Spanish called it. Christopher Columbus was the first white person to visit our island. It was 1492.

Alen:

There were native people living here back then. Columbus killed nearly every one of them. After that more Spanish came. They brought Africans to be slaves. The combination of mostly Africans and Spanish gave birth to the race that I am. And I want you to know it.

45

MY SOUL

Toro:

Before I came to America, I lived with my grandparents and my brother. He's fourteen, one year down from me. Sometimes we argue and sometimes we are brothers.

I miss my grandparents. My grandpa—he's my soul. I can honestly say he's the nicest man I know, and I'm not just saying that because he's my grandpa. He treats the old wino on the corner the same way he treats the judge that comes to get his hair cut at his barbershop. With kindness. He had many tragedies when he was a kid. He had every reason to be angry. But he's the opposite.

He likes to work in his garden. I liked to help him. We pulled the weeds and talked. "Education is important," he would say. "Go from the house to school to the house. In between, play a little."

We lived in a house with a flat roof, a porch and many rooms. Each day I had to make my bed and help my grandmother. Her life is about the family and religion. We are Catholic. She'd say, "God gives us freedom to do good or do bad. Toro, there is no gun to your head. But you'd better choose to look for Jesus." I heard her, but I didn't always listen.

Alen:

I'm Catholic. But I believe in spiritism, too. The Dominican government doesn't like that religion, but I know I have a guardian spirit by my side always.

I lived in Santo Domingo, the capital, in a house with my two older brothers and my one sister. When I was little, my mother told us, "I must go to New York to support you, my family. After I have saved enough, I will bring you here." It was hard for all of us to live by ourselves. She sent us money, but it was not the same thing. Instead, my older brother gave me the rules. I would ride my bike to be away from his voice.

Sometimes I feel I have always been lonely. I feel I'm stupid. But then I say to myself, "My life is not perfect, but then again, whose is? In my family we love each other, and that's what counts."

BOSS MAN

Toro:

In our country the men are the boss.

Alen:

And it's not so important to have a wedding. You can just live together. Women are about the home. Men go to work and give money to the family.

Toro:

But sometimes they try to find work, and they can't. They don't want to be half a man. They leave the family. I only know the name of my real father. I'm not curious about him, either.

Alen:

My father left my mother so many times I have six half-sisters and eight half-brothers I haven't met. It's the same with lots of people I know. Family members move back and forth from Santo Domingo to New York City. I tell myself, A child can lead what life he wants. In my heart, though, I know it's not true.

Toro:

My mother called me maybe every other week. "I want to learn the English language," I told her. I didn't tell her about my friend Ramon. I knew him for the longest time. He lived with his grandmother two houses away. He was always over. Then things started to change. Ramon spent time with older people. My grandpa said, "Toro, stay away from him." I did and I didn't.

Whenever the school said I was getting in trouble, my grandpa wouldn't hear it. He said, "Don't talk bad about my grandson. He's a good boy and he'll get through this." He believed in me and that's why it hurt so much when I let him down. I hope I can learn forgiveness from him. That's a hard one.

MY MOTHER THE STRANGER

Toro:

This year on Dominican Independence Day, February 27, my mother calls me. She says, "Toro, I am preparing the papers and passport for you and your brother." This is our first real time living together. She is a good person, but she is a stranger.

She struggles with life. She has no education, so she works many jobs. She sold flowers on the street. She sold sugarcane. She took care of other people's children.

Alen:

My mother worked for five years, then she got on welfare for about four. Now she's working again, this time at a factory in New Jersey. We are all thankful. It takes her a long time to get there, but she does it. She worries maybe the factory will close and move to the islands. To the Dominican Republic where people will work for little money.

WASHINGTON HEIGHTS

Toro:

Me and Alen met in school. We both love rice, beans and chicken. It's a traditional plate. I like boiled green plantains with fried eggs, bacon and ham, too. Plantains are like bananas.

Alen:

And we both live in a part of New York City called Washington Heights. A lot of people from the Dominican Republic are here. We can go into any store and speak Spanish. I work at a discount store after school and on weekends. I feel proud earning money. I don't work to impress people. I have to help pay bills at home.

Toro:

My mother fears the drugs and the gangs. I know a boy who drives a man around for fifty dollars a night and a quarter bag of weed. He says it's better than any Burger King job. I say, "But every night ends in a fight. How can you look death in the face and keep dealing?"

"Before I was sleeping on a nasty couch," he says. "I like fast money. And my girlfriend doesn't have a problem with all the stuff I buy her."

I try not to miss my life before. I dream I'm back sitting on the roof of my house the way I did. I take my radio up there, maybe a beer, and make a party for myself.

Alen:

Remember how you can take fruit right off the tree, mangoes, oranges, lemons?

Toro:

Once I made lemonade to drink on the roof. I only had to buy the sugar.

Alen:

The best thing about the United States is the opportunities you have for life. Some days I don't think my mother has hope. She thinks things will always be the way they are now. I hope for a better future. I want to be a computer programmer or maybe a translator for tourists in our country.

Toro:

When I finish high school, I want to be a pilot. I feel at home in New York. There's always something to do. It keeps me on my feet.

Stories of Mexico

5

CULTURAL RICHNESS

No single voice can express the richness of the culture an immigrant leaves behind. In this chapter are a collection of facts and impressions recorded by freshmen from Teacher Academy, Edinburg, Texas. They live just this side of the U.S. border and describe their ties to our next-door neighbor, Mexico.

Mexicans make up the largest immigrant population in the United States.

Short

by Erika Yaneth Medina
and A. J. Villarreal,
drawing by A. J. Villarreal,
Teacher Academy

Even before the birth of Christ, people lived in what we now know as Mexico. Advanced civilizations such as the Toltec and the Maya flourished until the 1300s when a new empire, the Aztec, gained control and extended its influence through much of the land.

With the arrival of the Spanish everything changed.

In 1521, joined by the other tribes that feared and hated the Aztec, Hernando Cortés fought and defeated the powerful empire. Since that moment this nation has reflected the mix and not-always-easy marriage of two cultures—Indian and Spanish.

Stories...

by Ruth Gonzalez,
Teacher Academy

It all began when Luz and Herminia Gonzalez came to America in search of a better life. Along with that came starting a family. Their oldest daughter was Dolia. Dolia was a young lady who had a son—Alfredo, Freddy—who was her everything.

The Gonzalez family, even Freddy, were migrant workers, Hispanic Americans who tilled the soil for the food we consume. In Edinburg (TX) High School, Freddy became popular for his football skills. He always worked hard, set many goals and accomplished them. After graduating in 1965, he enlisted in the U.S. Marines and was sent to Vietnam. He went back a second time because, he said, he wanted to help the Vietnamese people. It was then he died saving the men in his platoon.

A year later Freddy was awarded the Medal of Honor. In 1996 a ship was named and commissioned the USS *Gonzalez*. He is a hero. He died for his country, although his family roots come from the Mexican culture. Freddy was my cousin.

United States Ship
GONZALEZ (DDG 66)
Commissioning Ceremony
Saturday, 12 October 1996

by Twila Josefina Splain Chavez,
Teacher Academy

My father is Anglo (white) and my mother is Mexican. My father is from Washington State and has both German and Irish blood. My mother is from Jalisco, Mexico, and has both Aztec and Spanish blood. I was born in the heart of Mexico, Guanajuato, and have both of my grandmother's names. I have blonde hair, blue eyes and fair skin. Yet my features are like my mother's. You could say I'm like an Oreo cookie turned inside out!

When I was about four, we moved to San Benito, Texas, for my dad's job as a merchant marine. It's a pretty small town, quiet during the day, but at night—that's a different story. It gets kind of rowdy.

There are many barrios—sections— in San Benito. I live in La Palma (The Palm), the biggest. At first it was difficult for me to live there because of my looks. Some people are racist toward white people. But then when they got to know me, they changed.

Here a bad problem is the gangs. One barrio is distinguished from another by a bandanna color. If you live in one barrio it is hard to go to another. When you grow up in a barrio, most of the time you grow up the hard way. Still, in La Palma you awake to the sound of cumbia music or the tempting aroma of breakfast tacos from Taco Jardin. There is lowriding, *pachangas* (partying) and the strong unity of family and friends.

by Omar Montalvo,
Teacher Academy

I drew a comic strip, "Escape from Reynosa," starring my grandpa's parents and Pancho Villa. Pancho Villa was a famous Mexican bandit who stole all their valuables. To be safe, they had to head to Texas. Here's the happy ending:

by Rolando Rodriguez,
Teacher Academy

My dad was born in a small house, my mom in a clinic—both in Mexico. They had to work all day to be able to eat. They are always telling me, "We didn't have a childhood like you do today."

Finally my dad came to the U.S. to start a new life. He worked as a mechanic fixing cars. My mom was a maid. On good days she made $5. Looking back they say, "It was a hard and expensive step for both of us. And we are happy to have Hispanic culture in our blood, but we are also very proud, son, that you were born in the United States of America."

by Ricardo Ramirez,
Teacher Academy

I live in Pharr, Texas, a small town near the border between the United States and Mexico. Most of my mother's side of the family lives or has lived in Mexico. One of my cousins who is my age, 15, recently immigrated to the United States.

I interviewed him about his school life in an underdeveloped village in Mexico. Both of us were in the sixth grade in 1994. Though our homes were less than one hundred miles apart, the differences between us seemed like the breadth of an ocean.

SMALL DISTANCE BIG DIFFERENCE

My cousin's day started at five in the morning. He would get up, get dressed and do the morning chores. He would feed the pigs, chickens and lambs. Then he would get water out of a well and put it into barrels for daily use. After that he would finish any homework and put on his uniform. Then he would eat breakfast and walk to school.

School started at 8 AM. Before my cousin could go to class, the teacher would check his fingernails, ears and head. If the teacher would find lice or any dirty spots, the students were sent home and could not come back until they were fully clean.

After the inspection the students would stand for the national anthem and the roll call was taken. Before classes were started, the girls would go tend to the garden they had. The boys had a small field in the back of the school, where they would grow crops. After this the students would wash their hands and class began.

The classroom was overcrowded and had no air conditioners. Windows were opened on hot days or classes were held outside. The bathrooms were located in the back of the school. They were small wooden stalls with a hole cut into the middle. Underneath the stalls were large deep holes in the ground where wastes were stored. Once the hole was filled up with waste, it was covered up and the stalls were moved to another location.

The first session of class ended at noon and the students were sent home to eat lunch. At this time the teacher would tell certain kids to stay behind and clean the classroom. There were no janitors. At 1 PM the students would return and they were inspected again. Classes were held until 4 PM.

After school my cousin would get home and feed the animals again. He would also clean the house. Then he would eat dinner, do his homework and take a bath. My cousin would go to bed at 8 PM, and then get up again for the same routine the next day.

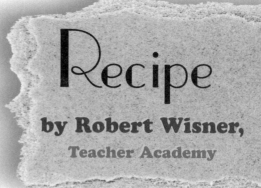

Recipe

by Robert Wisner,
Teacher Academy

During the long cattle drives along the Chisholm Trail from South Texas to Kansas City, the *vaqueros* (cowboys) would eat barbecue meat.

The trail boss would usually eat the steaks and the Mexicans would eat the fajitas (marinated strips of meat). Much later the trail bosses tasted the fajitas and preferred them to steak.

Through the years, fajita recipes have been handed down from one generation to another. Fajitas are usually the main course of a *pachanga* (party cookout). One of our family recipes handed down from Tía (Aunt) Panchita Quintanilla-Apache is my favorite.

How to Make South Texas-Style Fajitas

by Robert Wisner,

Teacher Academy

Marinade Mix
1 cup soy sauce
1 small bottle A-1 sauce
1 2-ounce bottle of meat tenderizer
1 teaspoon of lemon pepper
1 8-ounce jar of mayonnaise
1 teaspoon of mustard
1 fresh-squeezed lemon
½ teaspoon garlic powder
few drops Tabasco (optional)

Combine all ingredients in a large bowl and stir until blended and the mayonnaise is dissolved.

Meat Prep:
Place the meat on cutting board and remove most of fat with a sharp knife. Either leave the meat as steaks or cut the meat into 1-inch wide strips 8 to 10 inches long, slicing horizontally across the grain. Place the slices into the marinade mix. Mix with your hands until well blended; cover and refrigerate for two to three hours.

Fire Prep:
Heat the charcoal until it's gray with an orange glow. Mesquite charcoal gives a smoky taste. The ideal temperature is 350° F.

Cooking:
Place fajitas on grill and cook until they get a whitish color on top. The fajitas should be turned only once. Brown and serve. Sliced onions may be placed on the grill for added flavor.

The meat is placed on a warm flour tortilla. Lettuce, tomato and chopped onions with a spoonful of guacamole on top will complete the taco. They are usually served with a side dish of frijoles-a-la-charra (pinto beans) and Spanish rice.

Essay

What It Means to Be an American

by Arelia Montalño,
Teacher Academy

I'm an American. At first I was so proud of that fact I didn't value my Hispanic heritage. My parents are from different countries—my mother from Chile, my father from Peru.

My older brother was born in Mexico City. My younger brother and I were born in San Antonio, Texas. I lived there most of my life, twelve years to be exact.

I was ashamed of my parents. They don't know much English so I would have to translate for them. I hated this and would get frustrated with them. Sometimes I would deny knowing Spanish and was even embarrassed I knew how to speak it.

Then my parents told me we were moving to San Juan, Texas, in the [Rio Grande] Valley. I was mad. I didn't want to move. But when I started school here, I was shocked. Many students spoke Spanish. I thought to myself, Why aren't these people embarrassed?

Now after living in the Valley three years I have learned to speak Spanish correctly or at least to try to. I communicate better with my parents. I try to help them no matter what.

Most important, though, I learned from my Mexican and Mexican-American friends and neighbors to be proud of who I am and feel honored to have such an interesting background. And I hope others will realize they shouldn't deny their heritage either.

FOLKLORICO:
Cuentos de Nuestras Familias

The stories passed from one generation to the next are also part of a culture. And it is through these tales, the *folklorico*, that religious and moral lessons are often taught. Here are two popular Cuentos de Nuestras Familias, stories of our families.

Juan Diego and the Virgen de Guadalupe (Virgin of Guadalupe)

by Janie Guajardo,
Teacher Academy

When the Spanish conquered Mexico, their priests brought with them the idea of converting the natives' faith to Christianity. During the mid-1500s, they baptized a humble Indian boy, Juan Diego.

Juan Diego lived with an old uncle selling wood in the town. One day his uncle became ill and asked Juan to bring the archbishop for confession and his final rites. On his way to the pueblo, the Virgen de Guadalupe appeared before him at the foot of Tepeyac Mountain.

"Where are you going, my son?"

"My uncle has asked for the archbishop, for he is gravely ill."

"Return home, my son, for your uncle is already cured."

57

Juan Diego returned home, and to his surprise, found his uncle was well. Later that day when Juan Diego was completing his daily labor, the Virgen appeared once again at the foot of the same mountain. He was glad to feel her presence and her peace.

"Son, my wish is to have a temple built here. Go to the pueblo's church and tell them my wish."

Juan Diego rushed to the archbishop with her important message. But to his disgrace, nobody believed him. They asked for proof of the Virgen's visitation.

He returned to the same mountain, where he met her for the third time. Juan Diego sadly told her what had happened, and that he knew she was God's mother and his allegiance was to her. She instructed him to go to the foot of the mountain to bring her some roses.

"Mi Señora, it will be impossible to find roses at this time of year."

"With deep faith, my son, anything can happen."

Juan Diego found the roses for which he searched, and after presenting them to the Virgen, she told him to take them to the archbishop. He gathered them in his *ayate*, a special cloth, and took the flowers to the pueblo. Standing before the archbishop and the other priests, he uncovered the *ayate*.

To everyone's surprise, the Virgen's image was set upon it for all to see. The people present knelt before the cloth and the fallen roses, praying for the holy miracle.

Today the temple built is known as Basilica de Nuestra Señora de Guadalupe. It is at the foot of Tepeyac Mountain situated in Estado de Mexico, the capital of the Mexican Republic. Each village has its own patron saint, but this one, the most famous, is known as the Mother of All Mexico, La Patrona de Mexico, the Indian Virgin.

THE TRUTH ALWAYS COMES OUT

by Dalilah Vasquez,
Teacher Academy

Once there was a little girl named Maria. She lived with her mother and two sisters in a village so small that everyone knew each other. Maria's family was poor. Her father left them to look for work. After five years they still had not heard from him. Maria's mother raised her daughters, but she could not afford to buy them toys. The few dolls they had were shared among them.

Every night Maria would dream that she had a doll of her own, and every morning she would wake to realize she had none. Furthermore, she knew she never would.

In the morning, on her way to school, she would pass the marketplace. There she would see dolls for sale and the priceless Kernel Doll made of corn. They were beautiful and expensive.

One day she was daydreaming about a beautiful doll, when her friend Juanita came by.

"Hi Maria. Let's play."

"I don't feel like it Juanita."

"But why?"

"Because I don't have a doll."

"Maria, you know I'll lend you mine."

"I know, Juanita, but I want a doll of my own, like the ones in the market."

"Well, I'll leave then. See you tomorrow."

After Juanita left, Maria felt sad. That night, as she went to sleep, she promised herself, No matter what, I am going to have a doll!

The next day, Maria and Juanita walked to school together. As they passed the market, Maria showed Juanita the Kernel Doll.

"Soon I'm going to have a doll just like it."

"How?"

"I don't know, but I will."

That night while everybody slept, Maria sneaked toward the market. Suddenly, she heard voices and a dog barking, so she hid behind a tree. She started thinking about her mother telling her that stealing was wrong, and that bad things happen to people who rob. Then she thought, I know it's wrong, but nobody is watching; nobody will know.

Maria tiptoed to the store window and opened it. She was about to enter when she felt something walking beside her. She turned, and it was a cat. Maria let out a deep sigh and entered the market. She got the Kernel Doll and left without looking back.

By noon of the next day, the whole village knew about the robbery. Juanita came to Maria's house with the news.

"Maria, Maria, you didn't steal that doll, did you?"

"What doll?" Maria asked, then added, "Of course I didn't!"

"Well, last night, someone stole the Kernel Doll from the market—the one made entirely of corn kernels, that wasn't for sale.

"Maybe it is just lost."

"Maria, the owner said he closed the windows, and when he returned, one was open."

"These things happen. Why didn't he lock the windows?"

"Maria! Everybody here knows each other. Nothing like this has ever happened!"

"What are they going to do to the robber?"

"I don't know. My mom sent me outside so I couldn't listen anymore, but I know that whoever did it is in big trouble."

After Juanita left, Maria got scared. She didn't know what to do, but she knew she had to hide the doll. When she was sure her family was asleep, she went out back and buried the doll. Eventually everyone gave up. No trace of the doll had been found. Maria relaxed.

Winter came and went with a lot of rain. When spring came, the Kernel Doll had sprouted into a field of corn in the shape of a doll. Soon the whole village knew who'd stolen it. You can guess the trouble she was in.

So, dear reader, never do as Maria did. Remember what you read: The Truth Always Comes Out.

El Día de Los Muertos, The Day of the Dead

by Joe Ann Perez,

Teacher Academy

To Mexicans death has a unique meaning, with roots in the native past. The dead, we believe, should be both remembered and honored. Once a year on November 1 and 2 we celebrate the holy day, El Día de Los Muertos, the Day of the Dead. The festival is pre-Hispanic in origin and can be traced to the town Mixquic, which means "death" or "near the clouds."

The day begins with the ringing of church bells and is followed by much celebration, music and food. Family members go to the cemetery to offer gifts such as candy and flowers to the deceased. A bread called pan de muerto made of flour and a little spice is placed at the tomb for the dead to eat.

Family members also set up a shrine for the relative who is no longer among the living. It consists of many things: prized possessions, favorite music and sometimes even the person's favorite outfit or suit. Pictures of the deceased with the family are displayed, as well as pieces of the deceased's jewelry. Death—and a skeleton—seem like figures on a stage, bringing back memories of the departed loved ones.

The day ends with more ringing of bells, and with a touch of joy, love and togetherness. It is a Hispanic belief that life has no higher purpose than to reach death. And on these two days especially, we share the conviction that we have built a bridge between the past and the present, between death and life.

TRADITIONAL MEXICAN HOME REMEDIES

by Melissa Galvan,
Teacher Academy

Folk cures are common in Mexican households—from eating *menudo* (tripe soup) for a hangover to the use of herbs as medicinal remedies. These cures were carried by immigrants to the United States and passed along to others by word of mouth.

TARA LANA (SPIDER WEB):

This helps you immediately stop a bleeding cut. Find a spider web, make it into a little ball and place it on the wound. In a few seconds the cut is much better.

CURANDO DE SUSTO (A CURE FOR FEAR):

This helps you stop being scared. Lie down in the shape of a cross on a bed. Someone else places a blanket over you. They then get a broom, pray and pretend to sweep you. They put the broom on your head and pray again. Next they remove the blanket and make you take three sips of a glass of water, each time saying, "en el nombre de Dios (in the name of God)." Do this three days in a row and it will rid you of your fear.

SAVILA (ALOE VERA):

This helps you heal burns. First go to an aloe vera plant and cut off a piece. Next place it on your burn. This stops you from getting a blister. To stop yourself from getting a boil, cut a square of aloe vera, put it on a gauze pad and place it on the boil overnight. This sucks up all the stuff in the boil and makes it go away.

The owl is often the symbol of the *curanderos* and *curanderas* (the healers).

Art by Amy Austin

QUINCEAÑERAS "15"

by Melissa Moreno,
Teacher Academy

A Great Celebration

Many of the Teacher Academy students wrote about the cultural tradition of the quinceañera, the celebration of a girl coming of age at fifteen. Here are excerpts from their accounts.

In the old Mexican tradition, before this day the girl is not to put makeup on, shave her legs or talk to the opposite sex in a relationship manner.

Because this is a great celebration, the cost can run from $2,000 to $5,000, at the least. Many people help economically. They are called a padrino, godfather, or madrina, godmother. The girl is also accompanied throughout the day by fourteen friends, seven damas, girls, and seven chambelanes, boys, representing each year of her life (she is the fifteenth).

At the quinceañera there is a church mass and baile (dance party). Here people dance to tejano, huapango, cumbias, quebraditas, polkas, and many other kinds of music. After the first three hours there's an hour when mariachi come and serenade the girl having the quinceañera. At this point people take pictures with her, cut cake and send their congratulations. After this is done, the dancing resumes.

Once the reception ends, everyone goes to the young lady's home and has more dancing, food, games and a lot of fun.

by Corina Contreras,
Teacher Academy

In my quinceañera my mother and father decided I should do it like old times. I had to get up and speak with a microphone to everyone about how and why I am thankful for my parents. You can also talk about your influences. I spoke about my older brother.

Every girl should learn something from her quinceañera. I learned that I have to appreciate my parents more. Some people think it's a waste of money. My parents did too until it was time for mine.

It brought my mother and me closer together. Before my quinceañera I only talked to her when she talked to me. I never told her anything about my problems with school or with friends. Now she is happier because I do.

Here are some of my expenses:

Church rental:
$40.00

Church decorations w/natural flowers:
$325.00

Plant for church:
$40.00

Reception hall:
$1,300.00
(Mine was at the
Villarreal Convention Center)

Flowers for reception:
$250.00–$1,000.00

Invitations:
$200.00–$500.00
(I got 500, and I ran out)

**Dance instructor for
damas & chambelanes**
$150.00 for two songs

Cake:
$400.00–$700.00
(Mine served 1,500 people)

Reception food:
$200.00 per cow
(I served roasted meat. For this, my
father killed two cows)

Rice, beans, sauce, etc:
$65.00

Punch:
$40.00

Mints, peanuts for cake:
$70.00

Doll for car:
$40.00

by Mayra Ortiz,
Teacher Academy

Planning a quinceañera takes effort, but it's fun. The first thing the girl does is list everything that's required. Among those

63

is a church where the girl goes on the day of her party to give thanks and hear a mass. A cushion is also necessary; it allows her to be comfortable when she kneels down.

She needs a place to have the rest of the celebration. It can either be in a casino or someone's house. She needs to buy a pink dress, pink crown, pink bouquet, pink shoes, and jewelry. Other things needed include the car (decorated), invitations, professional pictures and a camcorder to record every nice moment.

A variety of drinks is important to keep everybody comfortable. Traditionally only beer, wine and Cokes are served. It is also a custom for the quinceañera to toast her chambelane in a big goblet while the guests use small goblets. And music and the surprise present—to keep everyone in suspense—shouldn't be missing.

Once the whole day is over, the quinceañera goes to sleep and wakes up the next morning ready to face a new life.

I asked the students who had a quinceañera why they did it and how they felt about it. Here are some responses:

1. Now that my quinceañera is passed, I sometimes think I would have preferred that instead my parents had just given me the money. I really did like it, but it caused some problems. —*Vanessa Saenz*

2. My mom insisted I throw this party. Besides I am the only girl in the house. It is an old tradition we follow here in Texas and Mexico. It only happens once in your life. Be mentally and emotionally prepared. It should be the way the girl wants it to be. —*Vanessa Rodriguez*

3. My mom wanted me to have a quinceañera because she didn't have one. Nothing can make me regret it. Be prepared to make sacrifices. Do not lose your temper. All your hard work will be repaid that night, the best of your life and you'll never forget it. —*Luisa Ramos*

The girls whose names you see below also wrote about this event.

Marlen Salinas

Amy Jimenez

Eunice Guzmán

Jessica Garcia

Lesly D. Moreno

Denise Cruz

Lisset Vanessa Garcia

Sandy Mendez

Natalie Marie Losoya

Julie Lopez

DiAna Peña

Alie Garcia

Alejandra Banda

PART TWO

POLAND

RUSSIA

EUROPE

KOSOVO

BOSNIA

ALBANIA

CYPRUS

LEBANON

IRAQ

ASIA

AFRICA

LIBERIA

GHANA

NIGERIA

CONGO

ETHIOPIA

BURUNDI

INDIAN
OCEAN

ATLANTIC
OCEAN

SOUTH AFRICA

N
W E
S

Longitude 40° W to 0° to 60° E

6 Stories of Eastern Europe, the Middle East and Africa

DIVIDED LOYALTIES

What goes on in the heart of a teen with strong immigrant ties? How would you blend and balance two cultures? It's almost like being raised simultaneously by a birth mom and adoptive mom—both of them fighting over your love and loyalty. That is the dilemma these teenagers face daily.

Short Stories . . .

Manny

My parents were born on the island of Cyprus and came here in 1979. My whole family and I are Greek-Cypriots. I am very attached to my ethnic background. I went to Greek school for seven years, and I go to Cyprus every summer for two months. I know how to read and write in Greek.

Racism persists between the Greeks and the Turks, and I have witnessed many horrible events between us. I know a lot about current problems and politics in Europe and am trying with many others to pursue peace and unity among the peoples. I can write a book on all this. But the time I have today in the library is little, and so is the piece of paper you gave us to write on.

Thomas

I come from Nigeria in West Africa. I started school here in junior high when I was twelve years old. Today is my birthday. I am seventeen years old. I live with my parents, my younger brother and sister.

My sister was born here, so she's pretty much experienced in the U.S. culture. My parents don't understand the experiences I am having. They didn't go to school here. I want to live my life like an American, but they don't agree. It makes us all a little sad. They worked so hard to bring us here, and now they fear I am disappearing into a world that confuses them.

Michael

My parents are from Poland and I was born here. My mother came to the U.S. in search of a better life. My father came just because. I have been through a lot that no one can understand or explain. Times are getting worse and hard to deal with. My father wants me to quit school, get a job and earn money to send to relatives in the homeland.

My mother wants me to finish my education. I know for all the pain she has to endure, sometimes she wishes she had never come. But even though my father hurts her so much, she is happy, for she knows we have a future here.

Miranda Abdallah,

Teacher Academy, Texas

My family name originates in Lebanon. *Abdallah* means "servant of God." *Miranda* means "extraordinarily admirable." My great-grandparents immigrated to the United States with others from their village. As was the custom, they left their eldest child behind as a sign that they would return.

They settled in Detroit, Michigan, where my great-grandma ran an inn and raised their four children. Her husband, great-grandpa Abraham, and his friend worked together until my great-grandpa died. Then she married his friend who became my great-grandpa Abdallah. They homesteaded in Ross, North Dakota, started sheep farming and had nine children all together.

My cousins are mostly Norwegian. I am the only one of my family that looks like a Lebanese person, like my great-grandma and great-grandpa, and that to me is very special.

Leonard

I am from a country called Liberia. It is located on the west coast of Africa. My family comes from the Kpelle tribe, which is found mainly in Bong County. Most of the members of my family have graduated from high school and college. Did you know that Liberia was founded by former American slaves?

Sienna

In Albania my mother was a scientist. Here she is a baby-sitter. In Albania my father was an economist. Here he is a custodian.

AN INTERVIEW WITH A RUSSIAN IMMIGRANT

by Catherine Christine Cognetta

(Italian-Irish-Polish-Lutheran-Catholic)

Morris Middle School, New York

I left Russia in December 1994, when I was in eighth grade. I started school here a month later. They put me in a class where all the students and teachers were Russian. Only that language was spoken. I was afraid I'd never learn English.

The government in Russia is poor, and they treat you badly. The jobs do not pay enough money to buy a lot of things. And everything is overpriced: jeans cost $100, sneakers cost $200, a loaf of bread costs $5. We measure people and food in kilograms, not pounds and ounces. My favorite food is chicken and rice. We often use parsley, which not everyone enjoys.

The housing is different in Russia. You own the apartment that you live in. The only thing you have to pay are the bills for electricity, heating, etc., but they are expensive.

The crime is bad. The police will only take action if the crime is outside of the family. If you get abused, the police don't do anything. They feel it is none of their business. I was abused when I was in Russia. When we moved here, my family kept abusing me. But here the police do something. Now I no longer live with my family. I live in a group home with other kids who need help. Still I love my family. I wish we could be together and it upsets me that we can't.

Mussa

I'm from Sarajevo, Bosnia. Before it was part of the country of Yugoslavia. My favorite teacher here in America is Jewish. The same was true in Sarajevo. She never smacked us with a stick the way other teachers did. One time when I made trouble, the teacher made me take off my shirt. He took a whip with thorns and hit me three times on my back. When I lived in Sarajevo, we didn't always have food because the war was going on. Me and my uncle went hunting in the woods. We'd kill a deer. Sometimes I worried I might die.

An Interview with a South African Immigrant

by Jackie Perkins

(African-American, West Indian, Caucasian), Morris Middle School, New York

I was born thirteen years ago in South Africa. We left, though, because of political reasons. There were many terrible things going on and my father was in exile. The government then was far harder on black South Africans than on white South Africans. The police were allowed to shoot black people to death if they caught you doing something they didn't like—even if you didn't deserve it.

I was only two when I arrived in New York City with my parents and older brother. Left behind were uncles, aunts, grandparents and many cousins. My family speaks English, which we learned in school. But at home we speak Zulu, which is also the name of our tribe.

Boya,
Young Adult Media Specialist,
New York, New York

Imagine yourself a young foreign student with no working papers and a social security card that says NOT VALID FOR EMPLOYMENT. Imagine, though, that you have to eat.

Imagine coming from Ghana where the average building is only four stories and arriving one evening in New York City. You call the one person you know to pick you up at the airport. What you hear instead is a voice on an answering machine recording: "After the beep . . ."

How to Make Cassava Bread and Starch

My name's Richard. I'm from the beautiful African nation Congo. My mother died when I was little and left behind five children for my father to raise. He married again, but he also taught us all to cook. Here is my recipe for cassava bread. A cassava is a cross between a thick root and a potato.

Get a cassava, peel and grate it. Then get a cloth, like a dish towel, and squeeze out the juice. (Save the juice overnight and in the morning you'll have starch that you can use on your clothes.) Put what you have left of the cassava in a bowl. Add a bit of salt and agitate it by hand.

Get a pot or a flat metal plate. Heat whichever one you're going to use. Then take the cassava and spread it with a circular motion on the bottom of the pot or the plate. It should be about ⅛ of an inch thick. If there are any holes, fill them up.

The heat from the pot or plate cooks the bread. When one side browns—about 3 to 4 minutes—flip it over to cook the other side. Now it's ready to eat.

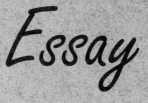

Essay

What It Means to Be an American

Summer,
Vashon Island High School,
Vashon Island, Washington

Being an American is something molded by the Constitution and the widely held belief that what you do is your prerogative, as long as it doesn't encroach on someone else's rights.

Colton,
Vashon Island High School

The idea of being a "real" American is very overrated. I think that being an American is no more special than a Vietnamese being from Vietnam. While it may be necessary to have a certain sense of pride in your country, it is equally important not to become arrogant and self-righteous.

I think that much of this attitude of being a "real" American began in the cold war. In order to rally the people against the Communists, the American government created an image of the "real American."

America is a country that has a lot of things to be proud of; however, like other countries it has a lot of things to be ashamed of.

An American is one who lives in America, and that is all an American is. There are many countries in the world that offer many of the same freedoms as the U.S., and some have better health care too. An American is a person just like anyone else.

A Longer Look:

Interview with Besama, a seventeen-year-old girl from Iraq

•••

Iraq, a Middle Eastern nation, is bordered by Turkey, Iran, Kuwait and Saudia Arabia.

I was born in Baghdad, the capital of Iraq. Now I am almost a senior in high school. Would you like to see my yearbook? I write for friends: "It doesn't matter how to fit in—what matters is how to carry on." They write in mine: "Here's my beeper number—don't wait for a Ricki Lake reunion to call."

DESERT STORM

I've been in the United States three years. People here don't know much about my country unless I get in a conversation and say I am from where Saddam Hussein is the leader. And the Gulf War—it's called Desert Storm here, I think—means something to them.

They were little. Often, though, they remember from television. For them the bombs falling was like a computer game. Not human life. They think we are crazy and mean and violent.

I tell them, "Iraqis are not ugly people. We're not prejudiced. We don't always carry guns. We don't like to fight all the time. Okay, sometimes we do have a bad temper. But that has nothing to do with the Gulf War." America went to war, I believe, for money, not to help Kuwait. It was about control of the flow of oil.

THE WRITING OF HISTORY

Before the Gulf War my father was an engineer. At the same time he was traveling and trading goods. We had real estate. My mother was a college graduate.

Back then, we lived in a house. My first time living in an apartment is here in the United States. In the beginning it was uncomfortable. Everybody could hear you.

In Iraq I shared a bedroom with my sister, The Spoiled Brat. At least it was a big room. She'd play with her stuffed animals, while my little brother was trying to take them apart and I was trying to study. Each neighborhood had its own elementary, junior and senior high school.

I'd go early and talk to my friends. We compared each other's homework and lives. We couldn't wear makeup, nail polish or our uniform skirts above the knee. The school was just girls. They wouldn't trust guys to be with us.

In fifth grade we started a second language. I studied English. In seventh grade we took a third language, Russian, French or German. I studied French. We had geography, too. I felt like we had to memorize every hill. In history, that's my worst subject, there were names and dates of wars to remember, especially in Islamic history.

Some say the writing of history began in my country. Maybe you've heard of Mesopotamia and the Tigris and Euphrates Rivers? I have relatives who live near what was a famous place called Babylon. We would pass by the ruins if we visited them for the big Muslim holiday Eid Mubarak.

After the Gulf War everything changed. There were no jobs. Food was expensive. There was no medicine. Men stood on street corners trying to find ways to pass the day and support their families. A difficult life could only get harder.

My father called us to his room and told us, "We have to leave." A month and a half later we were gone.

THE ISLAMIC WAY

Leaving the life we had was the worst. First we went to Jordan, a country next to Iraq. For six months we cried all the time. We didn't know anybody. My dad was gone, trying to earn money to get us to the United States. We all felt pain.

My parents gave me life. They helped and believed in me. I loved and respected them. My mother kissed each one of us before we went to bed. "We are together," she said. "That is what has value. Don't give up hope."

In the neighborhood where we lived everybody dressed in an Islamic way. Women kept their heads covered. They wore chadors, long dresses that go to the ground. With real traditional women, you could only see their eyes—no hair, no nose, no mouth. When they ate, they had to keep the veil over their face from getting in the way.

At first in Jordan my mother, my sister and I dressed more the way you do here in America. Strangers yelled at us: "The Qur'an tells women to cover their body from the eyes of men!" We began to dress like our neighbors.

Finally after eighteen months all the legal stuff was signed. We had saved a little money. We could leave on the last part of our journey.

THE PUNISHMENT

In my culture a guy can date and a girl can't. I've never even had a real kiss, a kiss on the lips where it means something special.

Here in the U.S., I hang out with guys and girls. I have more guy friends than girl friends. But still they're just friends. And I have all kinds of friends from everywhere. My best best friend is Arabic. My second best friend is Cuban-Chinese.

I was shocked when I came here. In my country, it's only Iraqi. Or before the war maybe some Egyptians or those from Sudan who came to work for two years and then went home.

I was shocked, too, by the freedom U.S.-born teenagers have. If you're a teenager in Iraq and the police see you walking with a boyfriend, you are in trouble. If you make out in public, you're in deep trouble. Even if you're married, you have to have respect for religious values.

If you're not married and get pregnant, you get killed. That's the punishment. The court goes by the religion in making judgments. At those times it is hard for me to love my culture.

WORDS, NOT BOMBS

If I had stayed in Iraq, I had planned to go to medical school. It's good money, but it's a long time to study, just like here. But this year I took a law class. It was fun. We learned about a man named Hammurabi. Four thousand years ago he wrote a code of laws. It said that the strong should not hurt the weak. He lived in the part of the world where Iraq is today.

In class I got to know about my rights. Like, I didn't know about sexual harassment. Hello, that is against the law. Don't do it, and if you do, I know how to fight: with words—not bombs—as my weapons. Now I think I would like to be a lawyer.

A Longer Look :

Interview with Dyli, a twelve-year-old boy from Albania

• • •

Albania, a European nation on the Adriatic Sea, is bordered by Greece, Macedonia and Yugoslavia (Serbia/Kosovo).

My father is a man of courage. He is Albanian.

He was seventeen years old and living in Macedonia. Back then that was part of a country called Yugoslavia. Now it is a country itself. Well, one year before he graduated from high school, they tried to put him in jail just because he is Albanian. He didn't want that life. So he had to run from his country.

First he moved to Italy. Italy said he couldn't stay. Then he skipped to Austria. For two years he lived in a camp for refugees. That is a place for people from different countries with no home. There he met my mother. She is Albanian, too, from Kosovo.

My dad applied to come to the United States. That was, like, ten years ago. The United States said "No."

He wouldn't give up. He wanted freedom. He wanted a future. "I left your mother pregnant with you in Austria," he told me. "She went back to her country. I went to Germany. I had a plan."

His plan was always the same: to get to America. Finally he found out how to do it. In Germany you get a visa to go to Mexico. You fly to Mexico and stay a couple weeks. You meet some guys to pay to help you cross the border illegal to Texas.

"It was scary," my dad said.

All the time he worried about how much money it would cost. All the time he thought he might get caught by the American immigration police. "I suffered," he said. "But better me than you, my kids. Better to be in jail in the United States than have no life. It was worth the money."

For three months he stayed with an uncle in Texas. One day, though, the uncle said, "Go to New York City. There are more opportunities." So that's what my dad did.

He spoke Albanian, Turkish, Italian, French, Yugoslavian, but no English. It was hard to find work. He got discouraged. He saw homeless people on the streets. That scared him. He did not want to be there next to them. He wanted his dreams.

Finally he found work washing dishes. For ten hours a day he washed dishes in hot hot water. It was like he was cooking his hands. He didn't care.

Then it was driving a taxi, taking out asbestos from buildings, cleaning floors.

What was even harder was to get me and my mom here. I was a baby. We first went to Germany and then Mexico. We had to sneak across the border, illegal, too. My mom repeats this story: "Dyli, you cried and cried until you had no voice. The Mexican men took you away from me. They said you caused us all trouble."

They made her cross the border without me. That made her cry but with no sound. She met my dad and they were afraid they would never see me again. They worried and worried.

But then we were together. That is all I know of the story.

No Green Card

Now I am an older brother with two little sisters. Because they were born in the United States that makes them American citizens. But me and my mom and my dad aren't. We still don't have the papers. We still have no green card.

My dad tells me, "I don't want to be illegal. I pay my taxes. I respect the laws. I went to a lawyer. He took $5,000 from me to help us get legal. He did nothing.

"Trust people, but don't trust too much."

Thanks to Allah

I am Muslim. In my religion you should pray five times a day. If you can't, you have a rope of beads to say prayers to make it up. You feel better when you pray.

Right now it is almost time for Ramadan. During that time, you fast. You can only eat before sunrise and after sunset. And you can never eat pork. You stay hungry for thirty days.

At my middle school in Brooklyn, we have a group of students that don't eat lunch. We stay in the library and do it together.

Sometimes my stomach hurts and I think about my favorite food that my mother makes. She takes bread, stretches it out and puts spinach or meat or feta cheese on it. She puts it in the oven and cooks it until it tastes delicious.

For Ramadan you go to the mosque, too, and pray some more. You give thanks to Allah and the prophet Muhammad. The women and the men are divided. If the mosque has two floors, the women are on top and the men are on the bottom. If it has one floor, they have a wall or a screen dividing them. It's no good if they aren't divided.

On the last day of the month, there is a big festival. Eid al-Fitr it's called. You have lots of food and sweets, you pray and you get money. If you're a kid my age, you feel like a prince. It's fun.

But my family celebrates Christmas, too. "We live here now," my dad says. "We can't be separate from America."

RESPECT THIS GREAT NATION

My mom tells me stories of Albania and Kosovo.

I'm not sure, but I think the people from Serbia come to Kosovo. "Give up all your guns," they say.

Then they start a war and Kosovo has nothing to use against them. They fight with swords and rocks. They don't have, like, automatic weapons.

People get killed. Friends get killed.

The Serbians set villages on fire. I hear my mom and dad talk. I hear the words *Kosovo* and *trouble*. I don't speak much Albanian. My parents say, "We should speak it in the home. We should not forget where we come from."

They want me to know, too, that Albanians are just one small population. We didn't have any freedom at all. But America, it is a free country. We should go to school to have a better life. We should respect this great nation, the United States.

And I do. I do.

A Longer Look :

Interview with Halima, a sixteen-year-old girl from Ethiopia

● ● ●

Ethiopia, an East African nation, is surrounded by Sudan, Kenya, Somalia, Djibouti and Eritrea.

I didn't come to the United States to stay forever. I came to visit my sister. To be a tourist. Together we looked at the Empire State Building in New York City, the Capitol in Washington, D.C. My sister had just finished her studies to be a medical doctor.

That was now two years ago. Once here, I learned something was changing with the government in Ethiopia, my country. One of my brothers and an uncle had big positions in an organization the government didn't like.

The government started to suspend the rights of my family. My brothers and uncle couldn't leave. My sister tells me, "Halima, you, me, none of us can go back to our homeland until the government changes."

"And when is that?" I ask.

"Nobody knows for sure. Someday."

I write letters home, but only half the time they get through. Most often they disappear.

QUEEN OF SHEBA

I feel scared and uncomfortable being in another nation. It is a different fear from that I felt in my country. We lived in Addis Ababa. That is the capital and it has many people. I think more than two million.

Ethiopia is in northeast Africa. It's an independent country. The main language is Amharic. In the United States no one knows my country. Well, one student said, "Is that where it never rains and people starve to death?"

How do I answer? Sometimes there are long times with no rain. People die. But Ethiopia is the land of the Queen of Sheba. In history it says she once ruled us. The last emperor was Haile Selassie. My father was high up in his government.

Before I was born, there were strikes. There was violence. Haile Selassie lost the throne. Then he died. Later my father died. In some ways that didn't touch me. I never knew him as a real person. I was the youngest of many children.

The servants lived in the house with us and helped my mom raise me. That is what they did with my two sisters and three brothers. They would do housekeeping and cook, too. My favorite food was the traditional food. You ate it with the hand.

My mother expected all of us, boys and girls, to get an education, to help people, to get married and have children. I love my family and my country very much.

ENDLESS FIGHTING

There are a lot of Christians in my country. We are Christian. But there are more Muslims. We don't have problems with that. We have problems with the different ethnic groups, different clans.

They want their own country. They want their own government and it is impossible to do. Eritrea, part of Ethiopia, had a war that went on for who knows how long.

Some of the war was underground. We do know that it lasted at least for more than twenty years. Eritrea became its own country in 1993. Because of what happened with them, this has encouraged other ethnic groups to try to be independent.

It is going to be a life surrounded by endless fighting.

BLOWN-APART BODIES

When I was still there, life turned upside down. It was one of terror, like running with no legs. There was no police force. Anybody could do anything. There was no way to stop them, no one to say, "That is against the law." The people with the guns and the bombs had the power. They still do.

If I went out of our house, I didn't know if I would be safe. When I said good-bye to my mother before going to school, I wondered, would she be there at the end of the day? Only this last week, they bombed a market and a restaurant. Places they knew would be crowded with regular people.

Afterward there were blown-apart bodies. A baby's foot here. A grandfather's finger there. And everywhere blood, bright shiny blood. Nobody claimed responsibility for the damage. That happened when I lived there, too. This kind of war hurts the whole Ethiopian people.

Today my mother is living in England. One of my sisters is there with her. I have more family in the United States, but too far away to visit. We cannot be together.

I miss my family. I miss the people in my country. I miss the mountains. Some are more than 10,000 feet high. I miss the Great Rift Valley, the Blue Nile, the sounds of the city. I dream. I dream that my family is back together in Ethiopia.

But I live with the truth. My future, I know, is here.

A Longer Look :

Interview with Pierre, a fourteen-year-old boy from Burundi

• • •

Burundi, a central African nation, is surrounded by Rwanda, Congo-Kinshasa and Tanzania.

Most Americans—black and white—when they see Africans on TV, they think we are dirty, we don't wear clothes. I try to tell them what Africa is really like.

"Africa is a continent of many countries," I say. "I'm from Burundi, a nation in the heart of Africa."

It is in my heart, too. It is pretty with high mountains, rivers, the bush and Lake Tanganyika.

Until I was nine, I lived with my family in Bujumbura. My parents first met each other in a nightclub. My mother was a beautiful actress. My father was a trader of purple stones and wooden carvings. He was born in the nation of Gabon on the west coast of Africa.

He traveled to twenty-six different countries. He went as far as Pakistan and Taiwan and back again. We wouldn't see him for almost a year. He would send me things for school, like a book bag. For my mother he sent clothes, shoes and belts. My mother became a businesswoman, her own boss. She and her best friend would sell the goods in the local market.

When my father would finally come home, he would bring luggage full of gifts for us. I would miss him, but in his absence I didn't have to become the man of the family. I had a grandfather on my mother's side, uncles and nephews as close as brothers. We were raised together in the same house.

That was all right, because I am an only child. Sometimes it's lonely. Mostly, you know, it means the mother and father put all their hopes on your shoulders.

NOSE TO NOSE

Some Twa—maybe you call them Pygmy—live in Burundi, but not many. Most people are Hutu or Tutsi. When I was still in my country, at first people didn't bring up the subject, "Well, are you Hutu or Tutsi?"

Everybody knew the Tutsi ran things. Then the Hutu wanted more power. We heard stories that Hutu strangers would burn down houses. They would stop a car to see if you were Tutsi or Hutu. They'd abuse you, beat you, even kill you.

I was little. I thought only about my life and my family. I spent a lot of time with my grandparents. Together we spoke Kirundi. My first language, though, was Swahili, the language of the people.

I went to what we called a French school, a lycée. We had freedom. We didn't wear a uniform, just normal clothes. If we knew we were going to be late to school, we'd wear extra pants. They'd feel to see if we did that and if yes, they'd make us drop them. And then they'd whip us on the butt.

After school, we'd go home to eat and then play with friends. Usually it was soccer. I was good at that. I didn't care if you were Hutu or Tutsi. I didn't even know what was the difference.

Now my uncles say, "Pierre, you are Tutsi." The difference is the shape of your nose. If you've got a big nose, you're Hutu.

My mother would tell me that her grandfather's father was a king. That's what I like to think about, not the size of my nose. That is as stupid as judging someone by the color of skin.

THROWING COTTON

I was around nine when I came to the United States. My father came one year before us. I didn't think, "Oh, I'm going to a different country." I was just going to see my dad.

There were no white people where I lived in Bujumbura. My dad told me there would be different kinds of people in America and immigrants from other places.

I remember putting on a suit he sent me and getting on the plane with my mother. We flew from Burundi to

Belgium to here, eight hours plus eight hours. And then, there he was, waving. What excited me, too, was the escalator at the airport. I'd never seen one. I'd never seen graffiti either.

My father drove us to the house we would live in with his friends. When we got there, I looked out the window. I thought someone upstairs was throwing cotton. My mother explained it was snow.

When it rains in Burundi, it gets cold. But more like 64° cold. I had never seen snow. From my father I learned how to put on a lot of sweaters, a coat and a hat. After that I went out and played.

My mother said, "You can wait a week. Then you will go to school. I will walk you there. I speak enough English. Don't be afraid."

At first, though, I was scared. My mom said, "I'll come back to pick you up at three."

They put me in fourth grade. I sat by myself in the corner. The teachers came up and started asking me questions. I knew three languages, but I didn't know English. One month before we came here, my mother hired an instructor to teach me the different letters and numbers. I didn't get any further.

In two months, though, I started talking a little bit. When I got home, I would watch TV with my mom. We would look up different words in the dictionary. After a while, we'd act like we didn't know any other language. For a whole day, we would speak only English.

A MEDICAMENT

I would tell my mother everything. Even if I killed someone, which I never would of course, I'd tell her. My father I'd never tell anything. I was sad when my mother had a miscarriage. A year later, she had another and another. She was sick on and off.

A doctor said, "Your mother has cancer." I couldn't believe it. My father had a friend in his birth country, Gabon, a special woman, a healer. She sent a "medicament," a medicine bundle wrapped in a knotted piece of material. It smelled like the forest.

"Your wife must believe in its power to help her recover from disease," the friend wrote. "She must keep it always in her bedroom near where she sleeps. Do NOT open the medicament under any circumstances."

My mother did all that and went to medical doctors here. Nothing worked. She was in a coma for one week. I held her hand and said, "I love you." She couldn't move, but still I hoped somehow my words got through.

She passed away two years after we arrived. That was the first time I saw a dead person. I worried her ancestors wouldn't be able to find her. I didn't want her to be alone. My father said, "I'll take her back to Bujumbura to bury."

In Burundi a mother has a piece of African cloth that she ties around her to carry the baby. I used to suck my finger and hold on to that cloth. I found the one my mom used with me. I put it under my pillow to remember her.

FOUR WIVES

In Gabon a man can have more than one wife. My father says, "I think I should have two or three wives. I can have as many as four."

"It is not right," I say. "You know in Burundi we don't do that."

Then he starts talking about my mother's family. He says, "Pierre, who do you like better between her two sisters?"

I say, "I like this one. She's more mature. She's smart and finished college."

I didn't know that when he goes back to Burundi, he is going to marry her sister. That is tradition. My mother was the oldest. If the oldest daughter dies, to keep the family from breaking up, her husband chooses from her sisters or a relative. That means I—the child—won't get upset either.

My father watches a lot of the news. When he is gone, I watch it, too. We stay in a house with twelve rooms. All of my father's friends live there. I am the only child. Out of respect, any man friend is an uncle.

My uncles say, "Look, look, pictures of Burundi." I hear them talk about a war, but I hadn't seen the pictures.

The Hutus are killing their Tutsi neighbors.

The Tutsi army is attacking Hutu communities.

Everybody is scared of everybody. Everybody is fleeing. Dead bodies are everywhere.

"War never dies," says one of my uncles. "It is all around them again."

I turn my head away.

My father comes back two months later—by himself. He married my mother's sister, the one I like. But with the killing, it is hard to get her a visa. When she does get one, she goes to Thailand, but there's a problem. She's afraid to show the officials the visa. Maybe they'll take it from her and she'll be in Thailand forever. Instead, she hides the visa and tells them she has lost it.

ALIVE IN MY DREAM

It is three years later. I'm fourteen now. I've got friends here, some around this block, some where I used to live. We have moved four times since I came to America.

I don't play soccer the way I did in Burundi. I play basketball. I talk with my friends about the usual things: sports, comic books and girls. I could date, but my father says he prefers I start when I'm fifteen. Girls call me, though. Some even come to my house.

My father teases, saying, "Anytime you want to have intercourse, I will leave the house." He doesn't mean it. He tells my uncles not to makes jokes about me. I wonder, what would my mom say?

Here at home we mostly speak Swahili, but now I can speak English with no problem. My mother's sister, my new mother, still can't get out of Thailand to come to America.

In my dreams, my mom's alive. We live in a mansion with rooms and more rooms. In my life, I say to my father, "If I'm rich, I'll buy you a house right down the street."

"No," he tells me, "I am in America for you. After your school is over, you are on your own. I will retire to Gabon."

PART THREE

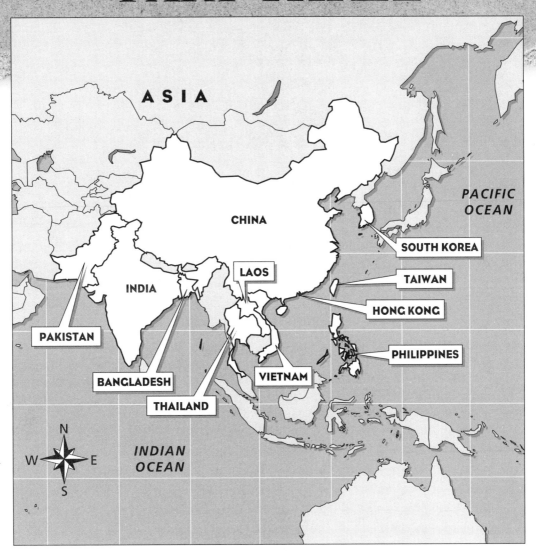

Longitude 60° E to 180° E

7 Stories of Asia and the Subcontinent

THE NUMBERS

Immigration is about people, not statistics. But to discuss and debate the issue, you may want to know a few facts and figures.

The United States has by far the world's highest level of immigration. Each year about 800,000 legal immigrants of all ages land on our shores. In addition an estimated 300,000 come here by other illegal ways.[1]

Nationwide 20 percent of children under the age of eighteen are either immigrants or the American-born offspring of immigrants. Their numbers grew to 13.7 million in the latest year available, 1997, from 8 million in 1990, making them the fastest-growing segment of the U.S. population in that age range.[2]

1. Bill McKibben, "Immigrants Aren't the Problem. We Are," The New York Times (March 9, 1998).

2. Celia W. Dugger, "Survey Shows Children of Immigrants Do Best in School," The New York Times (March 21, 1998).

Short Stories . . .

Michelle

My father sneaked out of China first. We don't have the right immigrant papers. He used his cousin's ID card. Ever since I was five, I dreamed of America. The day I arrived I felt like the luckiest child on Earth. My first job here I worked with my mom in a factory in Chinatown. She sewed pants. I was eight. I did whatever they told me. Maybe cut the threads that hang from the clothes. Maybe sweep floors. My goal is to be someone famous. I'm interested in singing and dancing. My parents say, "Follow the lead of your second uncle. Be a computer programmer."

Fernando

It has been seven years since I came here from the islands of the Philippines. My mind was filled with stereotypes from the movies and TV. I thought America had only white people who were very rich. In my country the people mainly live in poverty. Sometimes I used to fantasize about being a person of a different race. Dye my hair and get blue contact lenses. But now I realize my heritage is special. As I go through my family album, I notice that my mother wrote about her family tree and my father's. Even though I am Filipino, I have ancestors from China, Spain and Malaysia in Southeast Asia.

Seema

I came here from Pakistan when I was seven. I'm 11 now. We speak Urdu at home. But lately even though I understand everything, I am forgetting words. I wonder, am I forgetting my traditions, too?

John

I'm from Bangkok, Thailand. It is a wonderful but polluted, traffic-jammed city. Near the river is a king's palace that looks better than Disneyland. To show respect you have to take your shoes off when you go in the religious parts.

Here I live in an apartment with my pregnant mom, dad and little brother. My mom started throwing up and making weird noises. As soon as I heard them, I knew. This is exciting for my family—the first of us to be born in the United States. My brother is a pain in the neck. I share a bed with him. He sleeps like a dog and takes all the room.

Lam

I was born in Vietnam. I immigrated to Hong Kong when I was three years old, and I got here when I was ten. My father left us. My mother works hard to get a better life for me and my sister. I believe I'm not like other teenagers. I don't drink, cut class, smoke or stay out late at night.

Kelly

In China I lived in a poor village. My family raised chickens, but not that many. It's like having a kitty here. I knew which chickens were mine. My way of calling them was to make my lips like a kiss and squeak.

When I went to school, we did exercises first. If we were late, we were in big trouble. If we talked in class, we had to hit ourselves in the mouth—hard—ten times.

By eleven or twelve years old, we started skipping school to look for work. We work for money for survival, not to save. We never seem to have extra money. My mom would whisper to me, "I most like to sit and knit and talk to people." Of course, that was a dream.

Annie

I was born in Bangladesh, and I stayed there for thirteen years. Now I am fifteen. It has been great to be here, and I hope I will have better years in the future. The problem is I don't have friends and I would like to have somebody to talk to. I talk to my mom, but it's different.

Stanley

My dad was born in Taiwan, but my mom and I were born here. Still, sometimes people say to me, "Boy, you speak good English." Gee, thanks. It's the only language I know. My earliest memories are from when I was four. My dad standing at the side of the playground, watching me. At home he says, "Stanley, I am trying to figure out what you will be in the future. You are not a leader. But your art- work has promise." My mom tells me not to worry. Dad didn't know what he wanted to do until he was thirty.

Merrill Anthony R. Serenio,
Teacher Academy, Texas

Between 1700 and 1800 witchcraft and superstition began to spread in the Visayan region of the Philippines. Since then, the people talk about *aswangs*, vampires that fly at night, especially on the peaceful island, Antique (Antee-ke). This is an illustration I did of the "Legend of the Aswang of Antique."

Susan Zhou,
Midwood High School,
Brooklyn, New York

I was born in Guang Dong, China, and came to the United States twelve years ago. Times flies! I am a senior now. I love to cook, play sports, take pictures and travel. And I love living in the U.S. I love the freedom, the people and the best place to be—New York City. I live with my parents and my three very cute little sisters. One day I hope to own a business, make a lot of money and buy my parents a house.

Recipe

How to Make Special Spareribs

Susan Zhou,

Midwood High School,

Brooklyn, New York

Ingredients:

1 pound spareribs
1 tablespoon soft, preserved black beans
1 teaspoon of flour
½ teaspoon of cooking wine
½ teaspoon of sugar
1 teaspoon of soy sauce
½ teaspoon of salt
1 teaspoon of oyster sauce
1 tablespoon of green onion, optional
1 teaspoon of ginger, optional

Instructions:

1) Add the salt to the meat.
2) Cut the ginger and green onion into tiny pieces.
3) Mush up the black beans and add them to the meat.
4) Add the flour, the cooking wine, sugar, soy sauce and oyster sauce. (I also prefer to add green onion and ginger. Some people leave out those ingredients.)
5) Marinate the spareribs in all the ingredients.
6) Place the ribs onto a plate and steam them for 15–20 minutes.

Cool for two to three minutes. Enjoy!!!

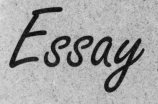

Essay

What It Means to Be an American

Margaret,
Vashon Island High School,
Washington

Our nation is not a village. We Americans distinguish ourselves by political party, region, opinion, economic class and religion. Little of our culture focuses on community or group efforts. In general, we are a self-centered people. Many of us lack appreciation for the abundance of good fortune. It is not until disaster occurs that people are willing to extend past their comfort levels for each other.

It is heartbreaking to watch reports of American life on TV. Hatred and violence are the dominant themes in the news. Some people rationalize that broadcasters avoid reporting positive events because good news doesn't excite the public. That in itself is disturbing. Do the American people thrive on the mishaps of others?

I think what should not be forgotten is that we are all very human. We work hard, we fall in love, and sometimes, yes, we suffer from broken hearts. The endurance of such hardships builds a nation of solid-hearted people. To be an American means, for better or worse, to experience life to the fullest.

93

A Longer Look :

Interview with Michael,
an eighteen-year-old boy from
South Korea,
and Clara, his classmate,
a seventeen-year-old girl also
from Korea.

• • •

Korea, a peninsula, is divided into two nations: North Korea and South Korea

Michael:

Last Wednesday there was a senior ceremony in the school auditorium. Clara got all these scholarships and awards. I only got a couple. Our families know each other. We go to the same church.

My parents smiled, but when we got home, I got the yelling of my life. "Clara's parents were so happy," they said. "Why can't you do that for us?"

I wasn't jealous of Clara, and I doubt that her parents looked at me with scorn. Anyway, she applied for those scholarships. I don't need a lot of financial aid for the college I'm going to.

I want to please my parents, but they make me feel discouraged and angry. I am the eldest son. In the Korean culture, with that comes responsibility. They want to see tangible results.

I'm eighteen years old and my father, especially, expects me to act like an adult. Still I'm not embarrassed to say that that night I cried myself to sleep. The next day, I talked to a teacher. She said, "Michael, it's not what you win. It's who you are. And remember, some students got nothing."

Finally, I just said to myself, typical Korean parents.

Clara:

When I graduated from middle school in Korea, I missed being valedictorian, number one in academics, by one point. It was all because I got a lousy grade in gym. I hated gym. I still do. I've never been good at it.

Before report cards came out, the gym teacher told us what we were getting. For me he said "Sixty." I went to see him afterwards, but he didn't care I was trying hard. When the grades came out, I was no longer number one. I was sad—and mad.

PRESSURE TO SUCCEED

Michael:

There's nothing I can do with my parents' pressure on me to suc-

ceed. Sometimes I handle it well, sometimes badly. I did bring home some track medals. That's something they can see. But in the Korean tradition education is valued so highly there's a National Teachers Day.

My parents teach me those kind of values. I will never forget them.

I was only three when we came to America. I have no memories of life in Korea. But in my home we speak Korean. I show respect for my parents. If my grandparents lived with us, they would have the final word. As the elders, they are respected the most.

I must also respect my teachers and those who are nice to me. My parents always tell me how we must cherish one another and those around us. Before I do anything, I have to ask their permission.

My parents expect me to be responsible, and I am. I know the consequences if I lie. Have I ever lied to them? Out of one hundred, maybe five times I haven't quite told the truth.

Clara:

In Korea most students are separated into all-boys and all-girls schools or classes. And the classes are bigger, as many as 50 students in each one. Instead of like here, where you run from class to class, we stayed in one room and the teachers moved.

Teachers assigned us specific subjects ahead of time. We had to take turns making up questions about the topic. We would come to the board and write them down, questions about math, English, history.

We lived in Seoul, the capital of South Korea, in a house with many other families. Sister and I shared a bedroom. We slept on the floor on a mat. At night in the dark, sometimes we talked about our dad. He left for the United States when I was six and Sister was five. "We have financial difficulties," our mom told us. "It's the only way he can support us."

GOD SAID, "DON'T GO."

Michael:

Ever since sixth grade, hearing about Desert Storm, the Gulf War, and things like that, I was interested in the military. I wanted to be in the midst of combat. As I grew up, I went to talk to an Army recruiter. He said, "Son, there's more to the army than just fighting."

I wanted to sign the contract to go in after I graduated from high school. I said to my parents, "I can get my bachelor's degree while I'm in the Army. I can save you money."

My mother wouldn't hear it. At night I heard her crying in the bedroom, telling my father, "In case there is war, Michael could die."

The elders in the church thought I shouldn't enter the military, either. I go to a church youth group every Friday night and services on Sundays. I had my parents and my church against me. Both are important to me.

Whatever I feel God tells me, I must do. I felt He said, "Don't go." The real me, not the rowdy one my friends see at school, is kind and mature. When I act up, it feels like I'm putting on a mask. It's expected of me when I'm with my peers.

I am a different person depending on the circumstances. I regret that. I shouldn't be a chameleon. I pray to God that He will help me show my true character.

Clara:

Ten years passed. I was sixteen and my mother said, "Our paperwork is done." After a lifetime of waiting, it was hurry up. We would leave in one month.

At the airport a friend gave me this cute diary. Right away my mom started bugging me: "Write in it," she says. "It's important to record and remember the passage of time."

After all those years dreaming of America, I hated it. In Korea starting in middle school, English is mandatory. I got good marks, but they only teach grammar and vocabulary, not how to speak it.

I couldn't understand anything. I didn't talk. I was afraid someone would laugh at my pronunciation. And they did make fun of me. I thought to myself, I was a good student in Korea. Here I am stupid. Finally I realized I had to reach out. To be a better speaker I had to be active and overcome my fear.

When a teacher gave an assignment, I'd find the unknown words in the dictionary. I'd memorize them and then do the assignment. It took me four times as long to study, but once I learned it, I didn't forget.

UNDER FIRE

Michael:

I have never dated. For four years I had a girl pen pal in Korea. My English teacher in eighth grade got us connected. We would write about life and our problems. She said I was the first boy she ever really talked to.

She sent me a picture from when she was little. I carry it with me—for moral support. Whenever I look at it, I feel happy.

I'll be expected to marry a Korean girl. My dad also says, "Marry someone at least three years younger. The younger must understand the elder has absolute authority. You know your mother is six years younger than I am." My pen pal and I were only twenty days apart in age.

I would like to marry a girl of a different race. Last month I told my mother, "I want to go out with a Jamaican girl from school."

"If you ever do that, I'll get your bags and throw you out."

My dad came into the room right then. "What's this about?" he wanted to know. When he heard, he said, "I'll be damned if I ever hear you went out with one of them."

"She's a devoted Christian, a valuable person," I said. "And she's two years younger than me."

"If people from different cultures go out, they argue. The household will be under fire," said my mother.

Inside I was hurt. "I know you're saying that because you are prejudiced against black people," I said. But they both said no. I wanted to yell, "There are Korean scum out there, too!"

Korea is known as the Hermit Kingdom. They want to isolate themselves from other cultures and keep pure.

Clara:

I'd been in the United States for two years, when I had to take the SATs. I bought a review book. I wrote down vocabulary on 200 index cards and brought them with me wherever I was. Meanwhile, my mom kept giving me articles about students who got 1600 on their SATs. I was proud of my 1310 score. My mom said, "Sixteen hundred would have been better."

When I was little I wanted to be everything from a movie star to president. But as I grew up, I realized that dreams are elusive. In fact, I didn't know for sure what I wanted to be.

Then I started thinking about my father. When we were reunited, he was different from my memories. He left Korea a young and strong man. Now he looked old. He had a limp, and that surprised me. "I had that when I was in Korea," he said. "But it wasn't noticeable."

"How did you get the limp?" I asked.

"When I was a boy, the fighting from the Korean War was all around us. We had to flee our home. I got an infection in my leg. An unlicensed doctor tried to heal it, by doing an operation. Instead he cut a nerve."

When he finished talking, I felt my heart was emptying. I decided I wanted to help people like my father. I wanted to be a doctor.

DO WHAT YOU MOST WANT TO DO

Michael:

We discuss my future. Recently I told my father, "I think I want to go into business—the marketing field." After we talked awhile, he said, "Michael, you haven't done enough

research. How do you intend to survive without being more thorough?"

I hate it when he's right. I do have to look into marketing more than I have. Then he said, "Go ahead. I respect what you're doing. In life, do what you most want to do." It was a special moment. I understood that a good parent also praises.

I wonder what my life would have been like had we stayed in Korea. Would I be a better person? Would I have had even greater responsibility to bring glory to the family name?

Clara:

My dad's a limo driver. I thought about limos the night of the senior prom. No one invited me. I didn't want to go alone or with my friends. Instead I told myself many things can happen if I never lose hope.

Near the end of the school year, all the seniors came to the library to get our transcripts. On mine was written number one. The principal called me up on the stage. He gave a speech about my average and the things I had done. The audience gave me a big round of applause.

I suddenly remembered how sad and mad I'd been back in my Korean middle school when I wanted to be valedictorian. The road from there to here has been an amazing journey.

A Longer Look :

Interview with Pang, a sixteen-year-old Hmong girl

• • •

These are a Southeast Asian people with no land to call their own.

My records say my birthday is in July. We're not sure, though. I was born in a refugee camp in Thailand. My family had been there probably for two years by then. No one really wrote down records of such occasions.

Sometimes my mom and dad talked about life before the Thai camp. Sometimes I listened. They called it "before times got hard."

THE PAST IS THE PAST

We are Hmong. We are a people without a country of our own. My parents lived in a village in the mountains of Laos. They were farmers. Their parents were farmers. I think their parents' parents were farmers, too.

I feel in my bones we are an old people. But I don't know how to count time. Storytellers, in a way, kept our history.

Hmong did not have an alphabet and so there was no written language until I don't know when. But not that long ago—maybe fifty years. No wonder my parents can't read or write. They had talents for the land, not for the mind. "The past is the past," they'd say.

And in the past the nation of Laos had a lot of political problems. Besides Thailand, it has other countries around it—a little bit of China, Cambodia and Vietnam. Hmong people helped the Americans fight the Vietnam War.

My parents didn't live in a region where there was much fighting. But when the war was supposed to be over, it got worse for them.

They heard that the Vietnamese were coming after all Hmong. They'd be sorry they'd helped the Americans. Hmong that didn't move fast enough were killed. My parents, my grandparents, my older brothers and sisters, the other people in the village started moving. Finally they crossed a river, the Mekong, to the Thai camp.

For me, it was the life I knew. Every day there was—*slap, slap, thwack*—the sound of women beating laundry on stones in the water. There were creeks near us. We didn't have to get licenses to go fishing. We had a dog. It seemed like there was no law. I think the Thai government ran it. I don't know. I don't even know how we got the food we ate.

In camp, there was a plot of land nearby. My parents claimed it and tried to farm. They only wanted some vegetables. It didn't help a lot. Once a week, meat was brought to the camp. They'd chop it up and pass it out to the families. One time someone tried to take too much and we all had to return our share.

I still remember.

THE RADIO TREASURE

What was my life like? We lived in long houses. Each had five families in them. There was the Yang family, the Vang family, the Lor family and so on. Those are their clan names. For Hmongs, there are about eighteen different clan names.

Each family had two rooms. One room was a bedroom for the family. Everyone sleeps together on a hard platform. Now I wonder how I could sleep on it, but then it was fine. We lay some of the blanket over it.

The other room was for cooking and living. The bathroom was outside. It was shared by the families. Sometimes you had to wait a long time or you could just go in the forest.

We had no bike, no candy, nothing electronic. Well, there were radios, but we didn't have one. My gramma did. It was a treasure. We had to be very good and there had to be special occasions before we could listen to it.

My parents didn't like our life there. They wanted to go back to the place they were used to. To the mountains. We were in the flat and dry land in Thailand. They talked of before, of farming and of hunting for forest animals—wild pig, squirrel, monkey.

They tried to think, How can we get money to raise a family? We had some relatives in America. They sent us money, but there was never much. My dad went to this place, like immigration registration, so we could come to America, too. They said okay, but he had to promise he'd pay the money back for the plane flight. He promised.

TOOTH-BRUSHING LESSONS

They moved us to a second camp. They told us, "Here we teach you a better understanding of American life." They had the kids go to school. I was six, old enough, but they didn't let me.

I had an ear infection. I couldn't hear well right then. They wouldn't even let me into the school grounds. I was put in a place for people they thought had mental problems.

I remember thinking, Man, I don't belong here. Mainly they made us draw and play sports. Oh, and they made us brush our teeth. That was the first time ever I had done that. I thought it was strange. They had a big tub of water. Everyone had a cup. They gave us a toothbrush and toothpaste. I drank the water with the toothpaste in it.

I didn't know what was going on.

My brothers and sisters were learning the alphabet. One teacher had them sleep during the day to get used to the sleeping hours in America. If anyone moved or talked, they were hit with a stick.

One day they called our name. It seemed like in minutes we vanished. We rode a bus to a big Thai city and next we got on an airplane. I threw up. I think it

was the flight. It was nothing I could even make up in my dreams.

PAVED ROADS AND GROCERY STORES

We came to Minnesota because my uncle came here. He was following his wife's side of the family. They had an American sponsor, a church group. The Hmong Association helped us get a house. They filled out legal papers with us. They made appointments for us to see doctors and things like that.

I was amazed by how big the city was. I was scared, too. It was the first time I had seen that many people. I had never been in a car. I had never seen frozen food, an inside toilet, a washing machine, paper clips. I could fill a whole page. The clothes were different, too.

In camp I wore a skirt and sandals all the time. My father wore Hmong pants, kind of baggy. I thought everything here was cool compared to Thailand.

Of course, I had to go to school. I was excited, but I didn't know what it was. They put me in first grade. I didn't learn anything in the beginning. We got recess and I liked that a lot. But that was almost like a dream now. Today I am a junior in high school.

I speak almost as well as U.S.-born Hmong kids. I guess we're okay to each other. But sometimes they think they're a whole lot better. They call us FOBs, fresh off the boat, or MTT, Hmong Thai Thai for a Thailand-born Hmong.

My parents worry. They say, "It's violent here." They know what I know. Some Hmong boys are in gangs. I think it's stupid and selfish. There are fights. They say they are protecting Hmong girls. But I think they are looking for trouble.

AN AMERICAN CHILDHOOD

We are expected to obey our parents. It's not our house; it's our father's. And the home is private from the rest of life. To my thinking I'll obey my mom and dad as long as I think they're doing the right thing. If not, I'll protest. That's the American way. I want an American childhood.

My parents complain right back at me. "Pang," they say, "you have gone past the line between Hmong and America. We'll return to Thailand and take you with us."

I am kind of reckless and naughty. Sometimes I do things without telling my parents. We're not allowed to do that in Hmong culture. I believe the younger you are when you get here, the more Americanized you are. My older brothers and sisters act more like Hmong than I do. My brothers and sisters below me usually do what I do.

In my culture, we had a traditional courtship game. Each New Year boys and girls tossed a cloth ball back and forth to each other. If a girl dropped it, the guy kept one part of her clothing. If the guy liked the girl, they would go for a walk. A lot of marriages took place right after New Years. . . .

We sometimes still do this, but we leave out the walk part and we are marrying later. If I hadn't come here, I'd probably be married. My mother doesn't know exactly how old she was when she got married. She just knows she was young. That's Hmong tradition.

And so are big families. They're good luck. We say, "God gave you much." We kids can work in the fields when we are young. When we grow up, we must help out our parents. We carry the family name.

I have six brothers and four sisters. I'm number seven. The last two were U.S.-born. I wish I was. Then I wouldn't have to apply for my citizenship. I still have to do that when I'm eighteen.

After that I will think of my future. None of my brothers and sisters has married an American, but I may. Who knows. Some of them didn't finish high school. I want to. There are no fields to work in. Hmong must try to change.

My oldest brother works in a factory. Another one sells fruit and vegetables at a store. Two of my older sisters are married.

But Hmong people in America are mostly poor. I want to be a good American. I want more success—and not so many children.

102

A Longer Look :

Interview with Sujada, a fifteen-year-old girl from India
● ● ●
India, on the subcontinent of Asia, is bordered by Pakistan, China (Tibet), Nepal, Bhutan, Bangladesh and Myanmar, formerly known as Burma.

Before I came here seven months ago, what I knew was the parade of life on my corner: the neighbors, people selling this and that, beggars. My only idea of the United States came from *The Oprah Winfrey Show* and—oh my gosh!—*Baywatch* on the foreign channel Star Plus TV. I was scared of this culture.

In India our parents and older brothers and sisters give us instructions. Whatever our elders say, we accept, even when it comes to marriage.

Most people have arranged marriages. My parents did, and sometimes my mother talks to me about what will happen. It goes like this. When the time is right, a marriage broker goes to a boy's family. They say, "Is this boy going to get married soon?" If the answer is yes, they take information about him, like how much he studies. They find out what he wants in a wife. Maybe someone who is educated, studied in India and is good-looking.

Then they go to the girl's home. If the girl is educated and knows what she wants, she says it. Some girls don't know. They just get married. The marriage is arranged according to the boy's choice, not according to the girl's.

There will be a dowry for me. That means the girl's family gives gold, presents and rupees—our money—to the boy's family. If the girl is less educated and is not going to work, her family has to be more generous. The boy also gives some gold to the girl's mother.

PROBLEMS FROM THEIR HOMELANDS

When I started school in America, I was amazed to see other Indian students. They were speaking Malayalam or Hindi, the language I speak at home. (That is the language I also dream in.) It was like being in little bits of India when I talked to them.

Some boys and girls bring homelands' problems with them. Like, they fight over a section between India and Pakistan called Kashmir. A girl from Pakistan said to me, "The Kashmir is ours. India has no right to take it."

I said, "I am not the owner of Kashmir and I don't want to be part of that fight. We are in the United States. We should just be friends."

Friends.

Will I ever see my friends in India again? I wonder. They made autographs in a book for me. Now when I feel sad, I open it and read what they said about me. Laju, my best friend, wrote, "Dear Sujada, Before you even leave, I miss you!"

A FLASHBACK TO INDIA

My day in India started at 5:30. I got on the school bus at 6:30. The school is based on the system in Great Britain. All the subjects were taught in English, except the Hindi language classes. School never gave us lunch. We brought it from home.

My favorite subject was civics. India has history going back for thousands of years. We also learned about famous people in recent times, too, like Mahatma Gandhi. He fought for the freedom of India from Great Britain. But he never did it with violence. He organized people and went on fasts to win the peace.

Gandhi fought, too, for "untouchables" to have good lives. Not everywhere in India, but some places, the people believe we are divided into castes. Upper-caste people don't allow lower-caste people—untouchables—to sit, talk or worship with them. They can't even work in their fields. Gandhi said that should be no more.

In the United States, Martin Luther King Jr. used Gandhi's ideas.

CHICKEN CURRY

In India we lived with my grandmother and my grandfather in their house. One of my uncles lived there, too. At festival time she and my mother cooked a special meal, maybe chana shag, chick peas and spinach, along with rice and a hot-hot chicken curry.

The house smelled so good from the food. My father stayed home from his electrician job. My uncle and grandfather stayed home, too. My mother only worked before marriage. After that her work was the home.

Since I was a child, especially at holidays, I heard, "We will go to the United States." I knew that was our plan. I just didn't know when. My auntie and another uncle came here the year I was born. Right away they applied for all my family to come. They fought for all of us. During this time they had two sons. Then my auntie and uncle became American citizens.

A New Beginning

Three years ago, still another uncle came to tell us, "Someone is calling you about your papers." From that day on we knew we were going. It takes time, though, to get ready. Nobody goes to foreign countries from where we lived. There was no passport office.

We had problems about my father's birth certificate. We had to have our pictures taken. Then we had to go to another state for the passports and visas.

My brother already had passed one year of college. "I don't have so much interest in going to America anymore," he said.

"Think of your future," my father said. "There you can study, get a better job and help your friends, especially John, with no dad."

Sons follow the words of fathers.

Once we had our papers, we went back home to sell everything. I had a tape of an Indian singer special to me. I had to sell that, too. My parents didn't have much money, so everything and everybody helped. My father had a little pension he would receive after one and a half years. "We'll give you back your money then," we said.

Finally, it was time to go.

"First it takes three days on a train to come to Delhi," my mother told me. "Then we go on a plane to Abu Dhabi in the United Arab Emirates. That's about four to eight hours. From there we fly to New York. That is a seventeen- to nineteen-hour journey. It is terribly long, but at the end is our new beginning."

Our Parents' Dreams

I live with my mother and father, sisters, brother, my auntie and uncle and their children. We are in the basement. They are upstairs. It's crowded but nice.

It took three or four months for my parents to get jobs. It was upsetting. I heard them talk. "Did we make a mistake coming here?" my mother asks.

My father now works at a gas station. My mom got a job in an Indian store. She takes clothes out of plastic, folds and places them on the shelves. Last week, though, the owner closed it. He said his rent had been raised and he could no longer afford it.

My mother has tried her best to find more work. So far there is nothing. I hear her crying in the kitchen. My brother is stopping college for a while to work to get some money. So am I. I will do anything. I have an application to get a job in a Shop-Rite, Taco Bell and Pizza Hut.

In India I would never have a part-time job. That is part of the reason we are here. India has the second-largest population in the world, about a billion. People are trying their best, but not everybody gets work.

I am happy to be in America. I thank you for letting me be here. I am learning to be independent. That's the American way. I want everybody to be united. We should have love for each other. We should be nice to our teachers and our parents. We should study and complete our parents' dreams and ambitions.

A Longer Look :

**Interview with Megan,
a sixteen-year-old from
Hong Kong/China**

● ● ●

*Hong Kong was a British Dependency
until July 1, 1997, when it became a
Special Administrative Region of China.*

I am an observer. All my life I look at people, especially my elders. I learn from them. And then I modify their philosophies into mine. It helps me, I hope, become a better person.

FREEDOM AND VIOLENCE

My grandparents and my parents went through many obstacles to get to Hong Kong and freedom. My grandmother, my mother's mother, would say, "It was terrible," and then she'd look so sad. The Chinese government called it the Cultural Revolution. Millions of city people were forced to move to the country.

"We had to leave where we had been for many lifetimes," she told me. "Your mother was just a girl then. The family was separated. Food was scarce. People died."

After the Cultural Revolution my parents' families flowed away to other parts of the world. Neither came from rich backgrounds. Their educational levels were below high school. Some of my mother's family migrated to Indonesia. My father's cousin went to Australia. Another relative moved to Thailand. My parents met and found love for each other in Hong Kong.

They married and had many occupations. My father was a chef, a singer and worked for a bank. My mother did cleaning, was a hairdresser and sold household products.

After I was born, my parents worried more. "There are dangers in Hong Kong," my mother would say. "There are drugs and violence. We want to protect you." It was not easy, but we finally were able to move to America.

I was six. The day we left, my grandmother said, "Quick, Megan, go three times around the apartment to show your wish to return." I did what she told me, and then we were gone.

THE SPIRIT STAYS

People say I resemble my grandmother. Everywhere she went, I would follow. I missed her so much. After I sobbed for a year, my parents agreed to send me back.

My grandmother was not like her friends, the other little old ladies. Still

she'd say, "Chat with them, Megan. That's how you'll become who you are." She made me think. She didn't like to talk about the same thing over and over.

One day she took a piece of paper and burned it. Together we watched the ashes fall in a pile. "The paper is in another form," she said, "but the spirit stays." I wasn't sure what she meant, but you're not supposed to ask your elders questions.

I just listened and watched. She was a flower arranger. That is important in Hong Kong. She had many students. She always wanted to teach me things. How to sew. How to sketch. How to play the piano. I knew exactly what songs she liked best.

Most of our family is Catholic. Some are Buddhist. My grandmother was religious, but she would say, "You can believe in a different religion or even be an atheist. Just treat everyone and everything with respect."

She had faith in herself and faith in me. She encouraged me: "Anything you do, put all your efforts into it and you shall do well."

NO THOUGHT OF THE OUTCOME

My grandfather spent time watching television. I remember what the people in Hong Kong called the Massacre of Tiananman. At my school at that moment, everyone stopped teaching.

We were taken to the auditorium to see what was happening in faraway Beijing, the capital of China.

Student protesters were in the heart of that city at a large open square, Tiananman. They wanted democracy for everybody. Peasants got off work and joined them. Then others were drawn there, too. The protesters looked like our older brothers and sisters.

Some people said, "Young students haven't experienced enough to make this judgment. They don't think about the history of China, how the Chinese government actually influences and controls the public. They only want to march. They demonstrate without consideration of the outcome."

And then came tragedy. The Chinese government shot the people. I had no idea what went wrong. Still I didn't think it was necessary to have so many people die. Looking at Tiananman Square now, I have to say that the spirit of the dead students may remain, but I don't expect that democracy will come to the country anytime soon.

TURNING POINT

I imagine myself being in a room with lights everywhere. There is a vase, too beautiful to be touched. But there is no sign that says DO NOT TOUCH. The more I approach it, the more tension I feel. The question: Should I touch it?

Yes, and then I must live with the consequences. Nothing really scares me. With many people, if they hear a loud noise, they jump. I don't. I expect the unexpected.

I didn't expect that suddenly my grandmother was dying. She had cancer treatment, but nothing worked. I played the piano for her. The music didn't soothe me, but she would almost smile.

I had to be strong for my grandfather, too. He was a smoker. I said, "You shouldn't smoke that much." He quit for me.

I was ten years old, still a child. When my grandmother passed away, that was my turning point. I started to have trouble communicating with my grandfather. I tried my best to comfort him. But every day, I remember, his eyes were full of tears.

My parents said, "Megan, it's time to come back to America. You have a sister and a new baby brother."

WAIT FOR THE SUNSET

I was eleven then. I am sixteen now. As a Chinese person, as a person from Hong Kong, I run into the stereotype that we're all smart. But it's not true.

In the beginning I only wanted to let my mind go the way the wind blows. I didn't have role models. I didn't see myself having peer pressure. I believed the most genuine person you could be with is yourself.

I would stay in my room and stare out the window waiting for sunset. I'd listen to my music and read my books until I could recite the lines. I didn't know where I belonged. In truth, I felt I belonged nowhere.

I saw the video of *The Joy Luck Club*. It made me cry. I responded to the relationship between the mother and daughter. I decided it was time to reach out.

Sometimes understanding yourself is not as important as understanding others. I begin to talk to other students from different countries about how we are assimilating. Even if we speak different languages, we can learn from the best of each other. We talk, too, about personalities. Underneath it all, we are the same.

TRIUMPH

I want to know how other Chinese teenagers are doing in the United States and their attitudes about the two cultures. I am taking a survey. For example, how many hours per week do your father and mother spend talking, playing or watching television with you? And does what you learn in school conflict with what you learn at home?

I am not sure how I would answer all my questions. But I do know that now my parents are more familiar with me and the American way of life. They know I am maturing and believe in me. I am now a United States citizen. We all are, my father and mother, my sister and brother. My grandmother would say, "Megan, think about what's important, the future—and then wait." So I'm waiting, not for inspiration. Inspiration comes from inside you. I'm waiting for opportunity to come. I am more and less than my two cultures. I am myself. I know I will triumph.

Stories of the Past Meeting the Future

A NATION OF NATIONS

In 1790, fourteen years after the Declaration of Independence was drafted and the American Revolution began, the first federal immigration law was passed by Congress. Since that date, immigration laws have been passed and extended, changed and amended. And since that date, a certain percentage of the current residents have demanded that the Statue of Liberty's welcoming torch be extinguished.

The more things change, the more they remain the same.

Today's United States is a nation where nearly one of every five babies has a mother of Hispanic heritage. Increasing numbers of citizens feel no one label applies—their pasts are an intriguing tangle of cultures. Others know little about their family roots, and many don't care.

Still, others have roots that go the deepest into the American soil. They are Cherokee, Navajo, Sioux, and so on—nations of people already here for centuries before that first outpost of Europeans was established on this continent. The United States has been a nation of nations since day one.

Short Stories....

Erica Maldonado,
Roosevelt High School, Bronx, New York

My People

My people are my nation
a beautiful creation
the future of tomorrow
the better generation.
The Puerto Ricans, blacks, Dominicans
and Cubans,
Our other fellow sisters and brothers
combined together
you know there aren't
any others.

In the past we were ashamed
to let you know we were there.
Now we hold our heads up high,
we're not afraid to look into
your eyes.

We are not afraid to express ourselves
with a word or just a stare.

We'll step to your face and let you know
what's up.
So, you prejudiced people
got to give it up.
We're not in the past, we are
not ashamed, we'll let you know
"those immigrants" are not our names.

We've grown stronger, so,
give us respect, and when you
step to my people
you'd better step correct!

art by Patricia Mosqueira

Calvin

I was born here in New York, and so was my mother. My grandparents are from Trinidad and came to New York when they were about twenty. This was during the late 1950s. Their last name is Italian. Their ancestors were from Italy before that.

My father's parents were from East India (Bangladesh), but he also has in him the blood of Cherokee, African-Americans and the people of Peru. I don't see him anymore.

I am a person who doesn't depend on anyone. I like to do things on my own. But when I can't, I ask for help. I am a person with religious morals.

LeighAnn

I compare our family history to a pot of venison-lentil soup. My mother makes this soup, and it's wonderful. Most ingredients are known to us, but there are always a few mysteries. My grandmother on my father's side is unsure who her father was. Her mother was divorced, I think, and had an affair with a man who ended up fathering my grandmother.

My grandmother is very dark complected. Sometimes, she and a few of my uncles look African-American. It's amazing to me. I am blond and have fair skin. Where did I come from?

In my free time I make videos where I put pictures together to music. I did this for my grandparents' fiftieth anniversary this year. As I went through those precious photos, I learned a lot about my family: part American Indian, Russian and German.

Still, I feel there is a missing link in my history. I am a mystery, just like the soup.

Renton

The force of Hurricane Andrew in Florida tore the trees out by their roots. It destroyed our house along with our memories. All the photographs are gone, my great-grandmother's needlepoint, my grandmother's favorite dinner plates and on and on. Now whenever there's a thunderstorm, I'm scared. Those are the roots I think about.

Amarylis

I am American with a German mother and Puerto Rican father. When I was younger, I was teased a lot because I am too dark to be white and I act, speak and eat too white to be Puerto Rican.

It used to make me feel bad. Not because I didn't believe in mixed marriages, but because I could not understand why someone would object to that. At this point in my life, I see being multiracial as a blessing. I get the best of both worlds, Spanish and German!

art by Patricia Mosqueira

Peter

My race consists of five different nationalities. My father is Russian and Austrian. My mother is black, West Indian and Chinese. It's confusing sometimes because I look Hispanic and some people don't realize I'm not. Both my parents were born in America. I was, too, and for all the labels, that's how I see myself, as an American.

Ted,
Language Arts Teacher, Hawaii

I don't really have roots. I was born in the Midwest into a family of German origin, the remnants of which they had largely shed or erased. Early in my teaching career, my wife and I moved to Hawaii, where I have taught now for more than thirty years.

I have always been a haole outsider, and yet I have also been accepted into the wonderful multicultural mix of the Aloha State. I think I simply feel part of everyone's culture. I have never had one of my own so much as found one from the elements around me.

Alec

I am American—third generation, full-blooded. All I know about my family is our roots are in Russia, Ukraine and some other places. America is where I live. America is what I care about. I'm very nationalistic. I can't help it. I really don't care where I'm from, only where I am and where I am going.

Daniel

I'm an American Indian. My grandma is from a rural community in southern Arizona. My grandfather left where he was from, Cochiti, to marry her. They live on a reservation, an allotment of land that was actually the tribes' to begin with. There's no work on the reservation. It's a bummer. Our religion is kind of half and half. Everybody up there is Catholic, but our beliefs involve a lot of regular Indian ceremonies with the Catholicism. Spanish culture is mixed in, too.

Before we go on a long journey, we get blessed or we can't leave. We won't be protected. Once I took a trip to New York City. I sure needed it there. It was chaos, nothing like here. They will not talk to you on the street. I mean in Cochiti, if we stop, people will come up to us and talk.

In our culture men are dominant. That's all there is to it. The men are the workers. They come home and eat first. Male teenagers eat with the men. Women and children eat last. If an elderly man comes to the house, we give him our chair. We feed him, no questions asked. It's out of respect.

I live in the Albuquerque suburbs in a three-bedroom house with a converted den, living room, dining room, eat-in kitchen, office and a large backyard. My favorite kind of music is reggae international and slow heavy-metal ballads that have a meaning to them.

I'm a senior now, but I remember studying about Asia in junior high. I know quite a bit about Buddhism, also. The other day a group of Japanese tourists was here in town. The similarities in the facial structures—between us and them—were amazing. I have a feeling from what I learned that thousands of years ago American Indians' ancestors lived in Asia. When it was all land, they walked across to what is now Alaska and then down into the rest of the continent.

A Longer Look :

**Interview with Jackie,
a thirteen-year-old Menominee girl,
and John Teller,
Menominee culture teacher and
former Tribal Chairman**

• • •

*This is a message from the oldest residents
to the newest residents.*

Jackie:

I'm Menominee. Menominees have lived on this land forever.

Today I live in a house in a town that's part of the Menominee Reservation in the state of Wisconsin. I live with my parents. I've got three brothers, three sisters and two half sisters.

I have other relatives living here, too. But the one I loved most was my gramma. She just passed away. She was a good person I could look up to. She would tell me stories about when she was young, how she grew up and how different it was from now. Back then they were surrounded by trees and animals—and touched by the beautiful Wolf River.

"In the past," she would say, "we would pick berries and cook and fish.

We had to do laundry by hand. We didn't have Nintendo or even swings to swing on. For fun we played lacrosse."

I can still hear the voice of my gramma telling me this story:

The Wild Rice People

In the very beginning there was a bear walking at the edge of the Wolf River. The bear wanted to be a human. He asked the Creator, would He do that? And the Creator said, Yes. He turned the bear into a man.

The man kept walking and saw a golden eagle. He said, Will you come down and be my brother? The eagle agreed. They kept walking and saw a crane and a wolf. They adopted a beaver and she was the first woman.

Together they were the first Menominee on the earth. Menominee means the Wild Rice People.

NOT FEATHERS, BEADS AND TEPEES

I like to travel and meet new people. I know there are a lot of people who come from other countries to live in America. I would hope they wouldn't bring illness. But other than that, I don't mind. Overseas in some places they're having wars. The people want to be safe. Overseas in some places there is no work.

The people want to feed their families.

I would like these newest people to the United States to know about us, the oldest people. Maybe you hear the words Native Americans or Indians. Maybe you don't know that Columbus wanted to go to India.

When he first saw people on land, that's where he thought he was. So he called us Indians. He was wrong. You can call us Native Americans or Indians. But I like it better when you call me by my tribal name, Menominee.

If you have never visited us, maybe you think we are just about feathers and beads and tepees. That's wrong, too.

John Teller:

I teach the Menominee students that to survive and succeed in greater society we should know who we are, our history, our songs, our language. In our culture our existence includes our life before we're born, after we die and what's in between.

We've evolved, but many of us still hold firm to the old beliefs. We value generosity, courage, bravery and respect. And by that we mean respect of everything from the earth to our fellow man of all races. We try not to be racist. Instead we judge individuals by their character.

If we have established a firm self-identity, when things get tough out in the world or even inside on the reservation, we have something to rely on. We know we don't have to be just like every other American. We have the right to be different.

SPIRIT ROCK

Jackie:

If you came to visit, I'd have you meet my family and then give you a tour of the reservation, starting with Spirit Rock. "Jackie," my gramma would say, "a long time ago there were three warriors. They asked the Creator for different gifts.

"The first one said, 'I'd like a good wife and family.'

"The second one said, 'I'd like great success in hunting.'

"The last one said, 'I'd like everlasting life.' And with that the Creator turned him into Spirit Rock. To this day people go by Spirit Rock, place tobacco there and say a prayer."

Then my grandma would say to me, "If that rock ever crumbles away, there'll no longer be full-blooded Menominee on the reservation."

We are religious. We have what we call a Big Drum. It's like our church. Anybody is welcome. We sing and, every Wednesday especially, we go there to pray. We pray for the people in all the tribes in the United States and for anybody sick or having troubles.

John Teller:

We are a nation within the nation. I was the Chairman of the Tribe, which is similar to the President of the country. Today we are one of five hundred fifty-seven federally recognized tribes in the United States.

Essentially each nation is culturally distinct. We have a variety of home dwellings, folktales and customs. There are still three hundred different Indian languages.

The Indian folks first became American citizens in 1924. But long before that, we have had Indian warriors defending this land dating back to the Revolution. There is a strong sense of patriotism.

JINGLE-DRESS DANCER/CHEERLEADER

Jackie:

Each year we have two powwows where there are different styles of dancing. I'm a Jingle Dress Dancer. My grandma told my dad I should be one. It is an honor.

But you know what? I'm a cheerleader, too. I'm in volleyball. I take the basic courses just like other thirteen-year-olds: language arts, science, social studies, math, computer classes, music and gym. Oh, plus one more, the Menominee language.

I kind of date and my parents kind of know it. My dad says, "You'd just better watch out."

My mom says, "Try to date within our tribe. But otherwise, as long as he treats you right, and learns to respect our religion—I guess it would be okay."

John Teller:

For us the issue of immigration often makes us think of life on and off the reservation. Life can be hard here. Many people left for the economic opportunities outside. The federal government sponsored relocation programs. They wanted to get Indian people to mix in with the rest of the country. Back in the 1950s they even gave us money to leave.

Then in 1961 the Menominee Tribe was terminated from federal government recognition. Overnight, we no longer were a people. We no longer lived on a reservation. Congress turned us into a county. Through lobbying efforts, we were restored back to federal status. It was in 1971.

Today there seems to be some re-migration back to the reservation. But still we are not isolated from the rest of the world. Instead, the world is coming to our door. Let us learn from the best of each other.

WELCOME

Jackie:

I'm proud to be Menominee. I like to be with the women, cook the meals, take care of the babies, make the outfits. The men are the only ones who can smoke a pipe in our religion. They can sit by the Drum and women can't.

When a boy gets his first deer, he has to cut it up and share it with different people. There is a big feast with fry bread and meat, wild rice and wonderful cakes. Girls can hunt, but mostly we don't like it that much.

I think about my future. Sometimes I want to go into cosmetology. Other times I dream of being a lawyer. I walk along the Wolf River. They're planning to do mining near us. It will affect our lives, the fish, the forest. I wouldn't want that. I would like to help the reservation and help my people have a good future.

To the newest immigrants I say, "Compare what differences we have. But don't forget to look at how we are the same."

9 Immigration Today: Student Activities

FAMILY FEUD

Ask the next three people you see what they think about immigration today. Should the numbers of those allowed in go up, go down or be stopped entirely? Once here, what restrictions and rights should apply to newcomers? What requirements should there be in order for people to become citizens of the United States? And what about those people who are in the country illegally?

Then duck. You may well be surrounded by a war of words, sort of a giant United States of America family feud.

In this chapter are opinions, short stories, surveys and questionnaires— most contributed by students from Teacher Academy, Edinburg, Texas, and Morris Middle School, Staten Island,

New York. Students from Vashon Island High School, Vashon Island, Washington, and the Menominee Tribal School, Neopit, Wisconsin, also completed various surveys.

Compare your thoughts to what others have to say on this issue. Then find out whether you'd pass the U.S. citizenship test and personal interview that immigrants must complete successfully.

Now add in this information: A multiyear study, the largest ever, found that children of immigrants overwhelmingly prefer English to their parents' native tongues and have higher grades and much lower school dropout rates than other U.S. children. They also believed that this country is the best in the world in which to live.[1]

1. Celia W. Dugger, *"Survey Shows Children of Immigrants Do Best in School,"* The New York Times *(March 22, 1998).*

What teens think about immigration.

Voices from the Valley

by Gladys Silva,
Teacher Academy

I have gathered opinions about immigration from many people who live in my neighborhood of San Juan Circle. San Juan is located in the Rio Grande Valley in deep south Texas, about eight miles north of the Texas-Mexican Border and 60 miles [97 km] from the Gulf of Mexico. San Juan lies east of Pharr, along Highway 281. Our population is about thirteen thousand.

The major industries for the area are agriculture, import/export and tourism. The mild climate and long growing season support citrus and cotton crops. The pleasant fall and winter weather also attract many "Winter Texans" who come down to escape the cold conditions up north and to enjoy the many amenities. The proximity to the border makes it a gateway for trade with our neighbors. One of our best attractions is the San Juan Shrine, which now stands adjacent to the expressway. Approximately ten thousand visitors come every weekend on a pilgrimage.

Mexican migrant farmworkers are among the most economically disadvantaged people in the U.S. Many don't speak English, are often paid less than minimum wage and live in extremely difficult conditions including substandard housing without basic utilities. Despite that, their outlook on life is optimistic. While they are economically poor, they are spiritually rich, mostly of Hispanic heritage, with a great love of family and community. They bring to the quilt of U.S. culture a tremendous wealth of song, dance, poetry, acting and art.

Here are some of the many opinions I heard. The last one is my own.

I don't see why people are against immigrants. They are the ones working in the fields and most citizens don't want that job.

—Jessica Rivera

I don't feel that immigration should be allowed anymore. It takes away the jobs we citizens need.

—Yanira Silva

I immigrated from Central America with nothing. Now I own a house and a car. I feel people should migrate, if necessary, to better themselves.

—*Blanca Valenzuela*

Many of my neighbors have illegal ladies working as maids, and they are doing a great job. So if no harm is done, there shouldn't be a problem.

—*Angie Diaz*

I don't feel that it's worth risking your life to come here. For example, thirty to forty people were hidden in a cargo train and almost died of dehydration.

—*Alejandro Moreno*

I feel that immigration is wrong. Some ladies get pregnant and come here to have their babies in order to get benefits from our government.

—*Claudia Sanchez*

This is a country comprising people from many different countries. If it were not for their desire to migrate here, we would not be known as a "melting pot." We are a rich country because of all of these diverse cultures.

—*Juanita Martinez*

I don't think there is anything wrong with families migrating and giving their family a better education. And, for example, we have many Cuban and Colombian doctors helping people here.

—*Gladys Silva*

A FEW MORE OPINIONS

Two other Teacher Academy freshmen also surveyed people on this issue. Here is a summary of what they heard:

As long as the immigrants are abiding by the laws, there is nothing wrong. Once they break those laws, proper actions need to be taken.

—*Lindsay Whetten*

Everyone should be able to come to America, although they should have both a job and a place to stay. They should be treated fairly and without prejudice. And when they do get a job, they should receive the same benefits as someone with the same experience.

—*Matthew Bowers*

Short Stories

STORIES BEHIND THE IMMIGRATION SURVEY

Two Hundred Twenty-One People

On page 129 you'll find a thought-provoking survey that explores many of the related issues to today's immigration. The thirteen questions were compiled by seventh-grade journalism students at Morris Middle School, Staten Island, New York. They asked 221 people, ages ten and older, to write their answers.

The students even went one step further. They were willing to tell us about themselves. Below are a few of their real-life short stories (and favorite recipes), which reveal the range of ethnic backgrounds in just one class and the differences and similarities among them.

Tishan Williams

When I was ten, my grandmother adopted me, my six brothers and little sister. My mother was African-American and Cherokee. My father is Puerto Rican.

I love rollerblading, bike riding, swimming, basketball and walking. I also love shopping and traveling. I don't like sitting around being bored. I don't like when people pretend to be your friend, but then they talk about you behind your back. When I grow up I would like to be a pediatrician, a lawyer or a photojournalist.

Howie Klekman

I was born on Staten Island. I'm Catholic, Jewish, Italian, Polish and a little Irish. My favorite foods are Italian dishes such as ziti. My favorite TV shows are *X-Files*, *Sliders* and *Millennium*. My favorite game system is Nintendo 64. My favorite sport to play is bowling. Last time I went I had a ninety average.

Kimberly De Jesus

I am Italian, Spanish, Sioux Indian, Norwegian and Irish. My great-grandparents are called *Bestamor* and *Bestafar*, which means grandmother and grandfather in Norwegian. On my stepfather's side there's *Nono* and *Nona*, grandparents in Italian.

I'm proud of my heritage. I like pizza (but I hate anchovies), ice cream, pickles and alternative music. I love salad. I find myself humorous.

Jillian Laub

Both of my parents are fifty percent Irish and fifty percent German. I live with my mother, a registered nurse and my father, a newspaper publisher. I also live with my younger brother. I enjoy being the oldest and having someone look up to me.

The one thing I truly hate is when people make fun of others for being "less fortunate" or for being "different." I feel individuality is the most important quality in a person. This is my opinion and my opinion only.

Kelum Wick

I was born on Staten Island, but my parents were born in Sri Lanka. My religion is Buddhism. I am the fourth person in a family of four. I am interested in computers and am a bigbigbig *Star Wars* fan.

I hate when people think they are the best and say, "I'm going to beat you up." I want to go to college and then become a programmer for Microsoft or a game designer for Lucas Arts.

Miguel Escobedo

I was born in Mexico City and have two sisters. We are Catholic. I speak two languages. In the future I plan to learn French, Italian and Portuguese.

Things I hate the most are squash, drugs and snobs. When I grow up, I want to be a chemist, an attorney or maybe a marine biologist. Last but not least, my favorite foods are enchiladas and arroz con pollo.

Arlie DeMeo

These are photos of my German great-great-great grandfather Johann M. Keppler (1830–1915) and my Irish great-great-grandfather William C. Casey (1840–1923). I also have Italian, French and English blood in me.

My cousin adopted a pregnant Haitian woman who walked into her driveway and asked her to drive her to the hospital. Today her baby is five and the woman has almost finished college. They are now part of my family.

How to Make a Double Batch of Cookies

Stephanie Marcello

I'm American, Italian and German. I'm also a proud Catholic. I have a little sister, a mom and a dad. Some of the things I like to do in my spare time, which I have lots of, is play sports. A talent of mine is talking. I'm great at it. Well, maybe not great, but I sure do know how to talk for hours at a time.

Ingredients for a double batch, a few dozen depending on the size of your family and the size of your cookies

13 eggs
1 teaspoon salt
3½ pounds of flour
1 pound butter
1 pound of sugar (1 cup)
1 teaspoon of vanilla
13 teaspoons of baking powder

Directions:

Preheat oven to 325°F

1. Mix all ingredients in a large mixing bowl.
2. Take a small amount of dough and roll it out into a thin strip, then twist the ends together.
3. Put cookies on cookie sheet; place in oven.
4. Bake them until cookies are light golden brown.

Recipe

How to Make Sweet Potato Pie Filling

Harold Dollison

I was born in the U.S., but my mom's from Aruba and my father is from Grenada. I've never been to Grenada, but I once went to Aruba. It's hot and humid. I loved going to the beach there. My family is a big help to me. They care for me. They teach me right from wrong. I hope to go to college someday and run my own business.

Ingredients:

3 mugs full of mashed sweet potatoes (about 5 sweet potatoes, boiled first to soften them up)

1½ cup of sugar

1 teaspoon of vanilla

½ teaspoon of cinnamon

6 tablespoons of butter

½ teaspoon of nutmeg

5 eggs

A few tablespoons of evaporated milk

Directions:

Mix the ingredients and put into a pie crust. Bake them at 400° F until brown.

How to Make Fudge Bars

Roxanne Morrison

I am originally from a small Caribbean island called Tobago. I moved to the United States in August three years ago when I was nine. I am five feet three inches tall, weigh ninety-seven pounds and am full of love for everyone. I have brown skin, brown eyes and medium-length black hair. I hate being judged by my physical appearance instead of my intelligence. In the future I plan on being successful in the field of journalism, cosmetology or medicine.

Ingredients:

2 ounces of your favorite chocolate
½ teaspoon of salt
¼ cup of shortening
1 teaspoon of baking powder
3 eggs, beaten
½ cup of milk
1 cup of sugar
1 cup of toasted nuts
1 cup of sifted flour

Directions:

Melt the chocolate and pour it over the shortening. Mix well. Beat the eggs until they are very thick and lemon-colored. Add the sugar to the eggs gradually, beating well after each addition.

Combine the chocolate and egg mixtures and add a little flour. Sift the rest of the flour, salt and baking powder together. Add some of the milk and the dry mixture to the batter, mix and add the rest. Add the chopped nuts.

Spread the batter into two greased 8-inch by 8-inch pans, which have been lined with wax paper. Bake for 20 minutes in moderate oven (325°F). Cut into 32 bars, one to two inches big. These bars are especially delicious when iced with a fluffy frosting and topped with nuts.

Recipe

How to Make Banana Pudding

Pavielle Clara Smith

My father's side is mostly from Honduras. My father was the youngest of five and the only one born in the U.S. A lot of my mom's side is from Barbados. I have family all over the U.S., Cayman Islands and Honduras. I'm short and loud. I hate when people who don't know you say they don't like you. I hate when people whisper in your ear and it feels like they're blowing in it. I'm twelve years old and am an Aries. (I'm really into horoscopes and people's birthdays.) I like thinking about life on other planets and also stuff like vampires. I think that everyone should be treated equally, even if they are in another world!

Ingredients:

1 can condensed milk
1 box vanilla wafers
1 box vanilla pudding
2 containers Cool Whip
1 bunch of bananas
4½ cups lemon juice

Directions:

Mix condensed milk with vanilla pudding and Cool Whip. Set the mixture aside. Slice the bananas and place them in bowl. Pour the lemon juice over bananas and set them aside. In a tin roasting pan, layer the pudding, vanilla wafers and bananas. Top with Cool Whip. Chill the pudding for one hour in the refrigerator before eating.

Morris Middle School's Local and National Immigration Survey

Do-It-Yourself Survey

Please write your answers on a separate sheet of paper. Then turn to page 130 to compare your responses to those of others.

Age of person completing questionnaire: ___10–15 ___16–19 ___20–29 ___30–39 ___40–49 ___50–59 ___60–69 ___70–79 ___80–89 ___90 and over

Gender of person completing questionnaire: ____Male ____Female

1. Immigrants take jobs away from Americans.

1. Agree/Disagree

2. Immigrants should not be allowed in the country if they have a serious illness.

2. Agree/Disagree

3. Immigrants should be allowed to become a citizen by marrying a U.S. citizen.

3. Agree/Disagree

4. Do you believe immigrants are hard workers?

4. Yes/No

5. Do you know an immigrant?

5. Yes/No

6. Immigrant children should be entitled to a free public education.

6. Agree/Disagree

7. Immigrants must learn how to read, write and speak English in order to qualify to become a citizen.

7. Agree/Disagree

8. Immigrants should be entitled to benefits under our welfare system.

8. Agree/Disagree

9. Immigrants have made many contributions to the U.S.

9. Agree/Disagree

10. People seeking political freedom should be allowed to enter the country without green cards.

10. Agree/Disagree

11. Immigrants should have one year to get a job or be forced to leave the country.

11. Agree/Disagree

12. Are you an immigrant?

12. Yes/No

13. Do you have any friends who are immigrants?

13. Yes/No

Results of Immigration Survey

The survey on page 129 was completed by 364 people from both coasts and in the middle of the country:

Morris Middle School and other teenage students (age 10 to 15) Staten Island, New York: 49

Staten Island adults (age 20 plus): 172

Vashon Island High School students (age 10 to 19), Vashon Island, Washington: 69

Vashon Island adults (age 20 plus): 12

Menominee students (age 10 to 15) at the Tribal School, Menominee Reservation, Neopit, Wisconsin: 62

Not everyone answered all thirteen questions; therefore, the numbers below will not always total 364. Some people were confused. Others were frustrated by the choices. One Vashon Island teenager wrote: "This form is full of unanswerable black-and-white questions. Both answers or neither is the best way I could respond."

The survey results can be analyzed in many different combinations. Here is a start:

1. (Take jobs away)   Agree: 159   Disagree: 191
2. (Serious illness)   Agree: 186   Disagree: 163
3. (Marriage)   Agree: 200   Disagree: 154
4. (Hard workers)   Agree: 261   Disagree: 47
5. (Know one)   Yes: 245   No: 98
6. (Free education)   Agree: 274   Disagree: 79
7. (Fluent English)   Agree: 270   Disagree: 75
8. (Welfare)   Agree: 165   Disagree: 165
9. (Contribute)   Agree: 233   Disagree: 83
10. (Green Card)   Agree: 132   Disagree: 145
11. (One Year)   Agree: 160   Disagree: 155
12. (Immigrant)   Yes: 36   No: 280
13. (Friends)   Yes: 150   No: 153

I selected three questions—numbers one, eight and eleven—to see whether the answers differed with gender or age. Here are the results:

1. (Take jobs away)

	Male	Female
Agree	81	75
Disagree	71	113

Under twenty, male and female
Agree	67
Disagree	102

Over twenty, male and female
Agree	92
Disagree	89

11. (One Year)

	Male	Female
Agree	99	69
Disagree	72	85

Under twenty, male and female
Agree	67
Disagree	79

Over twenty, male and female
Agree	93
Disagree	76

8. (Welfare)

	Male	Female
Agree	75	91
Disagree	79	86

Under twenty, male and female
Agree	92
Disagree	77

Over twenty, male and female
Agree	74
Disagree	88

Citizenship Test

Fifty? Twenty-Six? Thirteen? Ten?

Before becoming a United States citizen, a person must successfully complete a test about the nation's history. Applicants are given review sheets of one hundred questions from which ten are selected. Write your answers to these questions on a separate sheet of paper. Then turn to page 133 to check your answers with the correct ones. Give yourself one point for each right response.

1. How many stripes are there in the U.S. flag?
2. Who elects the president of the United States?
3. What do we call a change to the Constitution?
4. What are the three branches of the U.S. government?
5. Who is the current chief justice of the Supreme Court?
6. What is the Bill of Rights?
7. According to the Constitution, a person must meet certain requirements in order to be eligible to become the president. Name one of these requirements.
8. What special group advises the president?
9. How many times may a congressperson be reelected?
10. If both the president and the vice-president die, who becomes president?

Answers to Citizenship Test

1. 13
2. The Electoral College
3. An amendment
4. Legislative, executive and judicial
5. William Rhenquist (at the time of this book's publication)
6. The first ten amendments to the Constitution
7. Must be a natural-born U.S. citizen. Must be at least 35 by the time he/she will serve. Must have lived in the U.S. for at least 14 years.
8. The cabinet
9. There is no time limit (at the time of this book's publication)
10. The speaker of the House of Representatives

Sixty-four students from Vashon Island High School, Vashon Island, Washington, took this test. Here's how they scored and a sample of their comments:

0 points:	4 students
1 point:	12 students
2 points:	14 students
3 points:	10 students
4 points:	9 students
5 points:	6 students
6 points:	5 students
7 points:	3 students
8 points:	1 student
9 points:	0 students
10 points:	0 students

Three students answered that if both the president and the vice-president died, the first lady would become president.
Two students wrote that the group advising the president were called "yes-men."
(One point for being clever?)

Citizenship Question and Answer

Aargh!?

Before becoming a citizen of the United States, applicants must successfully complete this interview conducted by an Immigration and Naturalization Service (INS) officer. All of the questions must be answered, even those the person might consider too personal or embarrassing. As you read these questions, imagine you are the applicant.

Naturalization Interview

INS Officer: Please raise your right hand.
    Applicant: (Still standing, raise your right hand.)

INS: Do you swear that the testimony you are about to give will be the truth, the whole truth and nothing but the truth?

Applicant: Yes.

INS: Be seated. Have you ever been arrested? Have you ever had any trouble with the police?
    Are you a member of any organization?
    Are you a communist?
    Do you believe in communism?
    Have you ever been a patient in a mental hospital?
    Have you ever been diagnosed with any mental illness?
    Did you pay federal income taxes last year?
    Have you ever deserted from military, air or naval forces of the U.S.?
    Do you believe in the Constitution and the form of government of the U.S.?
    Are you willing to perform work of national importance under civilian directions?
    Are you a habitual drunkard?
    Have you ever practiced polygamy?
    Have you ever been a prostitute?
    Have you ever helped someone to come to the U.S. illegally?
    Have you ever sold or used drugs?
    Have you ever made a living from gambling?
    Can you write in English? Please write a sentence in English: (The INS officer will dictate a sentence for you to write.)

INS: Thank you. Now sign your name here.

Teacher's Guide:
Immigration Simulation

A decade ago I wrote about recent immigrants in a book called *New Kids on the Block/New Kids in Town*. Since then, teachers and librarians have told me how they incorporated it into their classroom activities. Marsha Kaplan, a reading teacher at McKinley Middle School, Brooklyn, New York, made my day when she said her students simply were nicer to each other after discussing the stories together.

I hope you have an equally rewarding time dipping in and out of *The Colors of Freedom*. The two books, however, differ significantly. The first one is a collection of oral histories of eleven immigrant teens. This book is that—and far more. Instead of allowing readers to see the immigrant experience as "we and they," *The Colors of Freedom* brings all readers into the picture. It taps into an almost-universal curiosity about roots by asking the questions, "Who am I?" and "Where did I come from?"

To get you started on this awesome adventure, here are some suggested real-life projects and simulation exercises.

1. Pick a location that relates to immigration experiences—for example, a government INS office, a small business owned by an immigrant. Go there and write down, photograph or sketch what you see. Turn that experience into a story.

2. Role-play the INS interview questions and answers on page 134. Discuss how you felt answering the questions. Are there any you think should not be included? If yes, which ones? Is this interview needed?

3. Interview the family member who knows the most about your roots. Include the unexpected—for example, a favorite family recipe, a diagram of your family tree, a memento from the country of your origin.

4. Videotape an interview with an immigrant—if possible, a classmate. Find out about his or her life in the country of birth, the journey here and impressions so far of this nation. Include a range of visual material, such as maps, photographs and any items from the day of his or her departure.

5. Make a storyboard of one of the interviews in a "Longer Look" section of this book, as if you were going to film it.

6. Read, clip and discuss news stories that have to do with immigration and the immigrant experience and/or stories about the birth countries of the immigrants in the "Longer Look" sections.

7. Ask some of your friends and neighbors to take the immigration survey on page 129. Discuss the results, including how they compare with those in the book.

8. Interview a public official about the history of the neighborhood in which you live.

9. Divide the class into teams. See which one is first to locate on a map or globe all the countries that are featured in the "Longer Look" sections.

10. Agree to serve as a mentor to a student in your school who is an immigrant. On a regular basis make yourself available to answer questions he or she might have. Explain the intricacies of homework, grades, the cafeteria, counselors, school teams, the PTA, etc.

11. Answer these questions. Share and discuss your answers.

Q. If you could only bring one suitcase on your move to the United States, what would you pack in it?

Q: Why would U.S.-born students make fun of a recent teen immigrant? Would you do anything if you witnessed this?

Q: What do you think is the difference between the people who immigrate and those who stay behind?

Q: What are some of the cultural characteristics of Americans? What is valued? What are some of the holidays and traditions?

Q. What is your reaction to the essays entitled "What It Means to Be an American"? What would you write?

Q: What is your best advice to immigrants on how to learn to succeed in this nation?

For More Information

Books

Ashabranner, Brent K. Photographs by Paul Conklin. *Our Beckoning Borders: Illegal Immigration to America.* New York: Cobblehill Books, 1996.

Bartoletti, Susan Campbell. *Growing Up in Coal Country.* Boston: Houghton Mifflin, 1996.

Berrol, Selma Cantor. *Growing Up American: Immigrant Children in America, Then and Now.* New York: Twayne Publishers/Prentice Hall International, 1995.

Fadiman, Anne. *The Spirit Catches You and You Fall Down.* New York: Farrar, Straus & Giroux, 1997.

Greenwald, Sheila. *Rosy Cole Discovers America!* Boston: Joy Street Books, 1992.

Herold, Maggie Rugg. Illustrated by Catherine Stock. *A Very Important Day.* New York: Morrow Junior Books, 1995.

Hunter, Latoya. *The Diary of Latoya Hunter: My First Year in Junior High.* New York: Crown, 1992.

Kosof, Anna. *Living in Two Worlds: The Immigrant Children's Experience.* New York: Twenty-first Century Books, 1996.

Levine, Ellen. Illustrated by Wayne Parmenter. *If Your Name Was Changed at Ellis Island.* New York: Scholastic, 1993.

Lewis, Loida Nicolas, and Len Madlansacay. *How to Get a Green Card: Legal Ways to Stay in the U.S.A.* Berkeley, CA: Nolo Press, 1993.

Olsen, Laurie. *Made in America: Immigrant Students in Our Public Schools.* New York: New Press, 1997.

Perez, Ramon ("Tianguis"). Translated by Dick J. Reavis. *Diario de un Mojado/Diary of an Undocumented Immigrant.* Houston: Arte Publico Press, 1991.

Shaik, Fatima. *Melitte.* New York: Dial Books for Young Readers, 1997.

Shinto, Jeanne. *Huddle Fever: Living in the Immigrant City.* New York: Knopf, 1995.

Simone, Roberta. *The Immigrant Experience in American Fiction: An Annotated Bibliography.* Metuchen, N.J.: Scarecrow Press, 1995.

Watson, Mary. *The Butterfly Seeds.* New York: Tambourine Books, 1995.

Videos

Avalon, written and directed by Barry Levinson. Produced by Mark Johnson and Barry Levinson, Tri-Star Pictures Production. Burbank, CA: RC/Columbia, 1991.

High School of American Dreams, produced by Freke Vuijst and Tana Ross, A Green Room Production. New York: Filmmakers Library, 1994.

Mississippi Masala, produced by Michael Nozik and Mira Nair. Directed by Mira Nair. Burbank, CA: Columbia Tristar, 1992.

My Antonía, based on novel by Willa Cather. Produced by Victoria Riskin, directed by Joseph Sargent. Hollywood, CA: Paramount, 1995.

Out of Ireland: The Story of Irish Immigration to America. Produced by Paul Wagner and Ellen Casey Wagner, directed by Paul Wagner. Charlottesville, VA: PBS Video, 1995.

Websites

More and more groups are developing genealogical society websites to help people track down their roots. Here are some sample addresses to get you started:

Allen County Public Library (national genealogical collections):
http://www.acpl.lib.in.us
Ancestry: *http://www.ancestry.com*
Hispanic Genealogical Society: *http://webcom.com/hgsny*
Irish History Roundtable: *http://www.irishnyhistory.com*
Italian Genealogical Group: *http://www.italiangen.org*
Jewish Genealogical Society: *http://members.aol.com/jgsny/main.htm*
Lineages: *http://www.lineagesnet.com*
Library of Congress: *http://www.loc.gov*
Polish Genealogical Society: *http://www.feefhs.org*

With Thanks/Muchas Gracias/Etc.

This book would not exist if my ancestors hadn't begun our journey so many generations ago. I thank them for starting the adventure of turning us into Americans.

Thanks go as well to my extended family today: my sweet partner, Stan Mack, who listened to my retelling of the collected stories and provided invaluable guidance on the design of these pages; my sisters, Barbara and Carolyn, who share my memories of life, death and family reunions; plus Coach, Ernie, Frieda, Gloria, Kenny, Kerri, Peggy, Pearl, Peter, Stephanie and my numerous cousins. They are scattered across the United States but are still most heavily in the Midwest.

And, of course, I thank my family of friends, including Linda Broessel, Phyllis Cadle, Wendy Caplan, Lucy Cefalu, Jane Goldberg, Harriet and Ted Gottfried, Kay Franey, Carole Mayedo, Rosemarie and Marvin Mazor, San San Tin and my now-dispersed Third Thursday Group of Women Writers, especially Jane O'Reilly and Andrea Boroff Eagan, wherever she may be. (Thanks, too, to my assistants, Lisa Stump and Kathy Ebel.)

The following people invited me into their homes, schools, libraries and offices. They arranged for me to speak to students and recommended specific individuals to interview. They were all wonderful occasions. Thanks go to Gail Barraco, media specialist, Groton Middle/High School, Groton, New York; Iris Baum, principal/Marsha Kaplan, reading teacher, McKinley Middle School, Brooklyn, New York; Deloris Brown, English teacher/Sonya Geismar, media specialist, Roosevelt High School, Bronx, New York; Holly Cazarinoff, BOSCES—Ithaca, New York; Donna Chumas, media specialist, Patchogue High School, Patchogue, New York; Abdel Djemil/Marwan Khaled, Islamic Society of Bay Ridge, Brooklyn, New York; Katy Farrell/Kathleen Samsun, ESL teachers, Liberty High School, New York, New York; Janet Gelfand/Sybil Oster, media specialists, Lawrence Middle School, Lawrence, New York; Julie Jaffe, teacher/Clam adviser, Vashon Island High School, Vashon Island, Washington; Kaarin Kolbre, media specialist, Murray Bergtraum High School, New York, New York; John Kraus, journalism teacher, Martin Luther King Jr. High School, New York, New York; Harriet Rudnick, media specialist/Sandra Birnback, ESL teacher, Roosevelt High School, Yonkers, New York; Heather Rugel, ESL teacher, Locust Valley Middle/High

School, Locust Valley, New York; Jane Shoemaker, media specialist, North High School, Sheboygan, Wisconsin; Adah Silberg/Arlene Rio, media specialists, Peninsula Public Library, Lawrence, New York; Elaine Stephens/Jean Brown, professors of library science/(NCTE November 1997 Detroit Convention), Saginaw Valley State University, University Center, Michigan; Anne Valsamakis, Portland, Oregon; Paul Walsh, principal (and Mrs. Accornero, parent), William A. Morris IS 61 Middle School, Staten Island, New York; Arlene Weber Morales, media specialist, Marine Park Middle School, Brooklyn, New York; Bonnie Wojnowski, media specialist, Candor Middle/High School, Candor, New York.

I wish there were room to list all the students from Erminia Claudio's seventh grade journalism class and Patricia Power's ninth- and tenth-graders whose projects did not appear on these preceding pages. I convinced my wonderful editor, E. Russell Primm III, to allow me to create a far larger book than originally anticipated—but there are still not enough pages to include every contribution. My enduring thanks to you all.

Where in the World Is Janet Bode?

At age thirteen Janet Bode discovered there was a world beyond the United States. She lived with her family in England for two and a half years. Then in her twenties she worked in different countries, including Mexico, where she taught school for two years.

She's walked on the Great Wall of China, sailed on a felucca up the Nile in Egypt, explored the world of the Inca in Peru and talked with Aborigines in Australia's Red Desert. She's lived in eight states, on both coasts and in the middle of the country. Bode brings a unique perspective to the issue of immigration: She sees our nation from inside and out, emotionally and objectively.

The Colors of Freedom: Immigrant Stories is her fourteenth young adult nonfiction book. She lives in New York City—and most likely is packing.

Index

Numbers in *italics* represent illustrations.